The Handbook of Communication Skills

FRANK P. MURPHY

Managing Director,
Ireland's Institute of Communication Ltd

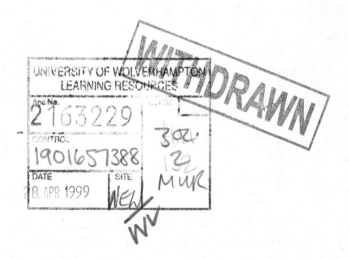

BLACKHALL
Publishing

This book was typeset by
Gough Typesetting Services for
BLACKHALL PUBLISHING LTD
26 Eustace Street, Dublin 2.
(e-mail: blackhall@tinet.ie)

A catalogue record for this book
is available from the British Library

ISBN 1-901657-16-7 pbk
ISBN 1-901657-38-8 hbk

Printed by
Betaprint Ltd.

Contents

Foreword

The ability to communicate is one of the great human gifts. Language in all its form and manifestations is one of the key elements that separates humans from all the other species on this earth.

But a very large number of people are simply incapable of realising their full potential when it comes to communication with other people. There are many reasons for this – nervousness, a speech impediment from childhood which has physically disappeared but whose legacy remains, or simply a sheer fear of making a fool of oneself when standing up to speak to a group or at a public meeting.

Many of those people look in wonderment and awe at people who can address a public meeting without any sense of nervousness or without reference to any notes. The clarity of the voice, the flow of the rhetorical phrase and the modulation in the tone to convey the range of emotions underlining the message all seem to be inaccessible skills which they could never possess.

Well, appearances can be very deceptive. Most people who have learnt to speak in public and who now use it as part of their stock and trade, such as politicians, have had to overcome the same fears, the same doubts and the same barriers that prevent many people today from communicating effectively.

Those people have been helped by attending communication courses and participating in the various classes and exercises, which such courses provide. Frank Murphy has been doing this for many, many years with considerable skill and a lot of success. His own story of how he came to overcome the personal barriers and limitations of communication is a solitary lesson and a great inspiration for people who want to overcome their own inability to properly communicate.

This handbook of communication skills is about far more than just the ability to stand up and address an audience. It covers the important areas of human behaviour, conflict resolution and how to properly preside over a meeting so as to ensure an effective result at the end of it. Likewise, presentations skills and negotiation skills are addressed. Taken together, the various chapters provide a comprehensive course in the art of communication skills.

Frank Murphy has been doing this work for many years. At last, he has found the time to set down in writing much of what it is he teaches during his courses. As you can see from reading the book he draws heavily from his own experience as a shy introverted young person and builds upon that as he chronicles his success in later life, overcoming his own difficulties and helping other people to overcome theirs. This is a very useful book which I know will help many people to improve their communication skills and so ensure that the message which they possess is properly heard.

Ruairí Quinn, T.D.,
Leader of the Labour Party

Introduction

The Communications Training Programme which Frank Murphy now conducts trains people how to:

- Become very confident and positive
- Become very effective communicators
- Remember the individual names of groups of people that they meet
- Stand up and speak in public and make professional presentations
- Think clearly when under pressure and cope with challenging situations
- Influence and persuade people to accept their ideas
- Oppose individuals in a constructive way

The sessions are participative with each participant implementing the skills that are outlined.

While listening to lectures on these topics is very interesting, it is taking part in the training programme that upgrades people's skills and helps them to be successful in both their working and personal lives.

The Handbook of Communication Skills provides an introduction to Frank Murphy's unique methodology in these areas and gives an insight into how to become effective in all areas of communication.

Acknowledgements

I would like to extend my thanks to the companies, professional organisations and government departments who have used the services of Ireland's Institute of Communication Ltd over the years.

The first professional organisation that used my services was what was then called An Foras Talúntais, now Teagasc. They have sent people on my courses since 1973.

Thanks also to The Institute of Chartered Accountants in Ireland, who appointed me as a Presentation Skills Trainer in 1984.

Martina Quinn, the Administration Manager of Ireland's Institute of Communication Ltd, did an excellent job typing up the manu-script.

Before I started operating from my own premises I conducted my courses at the Mount Herbert Hotel on Herbert Road, Dublin 4. It is an extremely good hotel and the people who attended the courses were very impressed with it. I would like to extend my thanks to the Loughran family who own the hotel for the support they have given me. I wrote a large part of this book in the Mount Herbert Hotel.

I would also like to extend my thanks to Elo Press Ltd, of Reuben Avenue, Dublin 8. They have produced a range of excellent brochures and portfolios for me over the years. I would like to thank Mr Patrick Funge, the owner of the company, and all his staff for the work they have done for me.

Frank P. Murphy
February 1998

1

Outline of the Book

This opening section outlines the purpose and content of this book and how and why it was devised. All of the skills that I possess have come from the practical experience that I developed in the many organisations that I have been involved in since the 1960s and from my study of psychology. I was never a facilitator presenting courses devised by other people, though I am not opposed to that. There are some very good facilitators. All specialists in every area have some things in common so it is possible that there is a similarity between some of the content of my courses and that of other communications training courses.

The reason why I studied psychology was that I had a lot of ideas about how human beings thought and how they should be treated. I was anxious to find out if what I believed was right. A lot of what I believed did turn out to be right. Also I wanted to go into politics due to the background that I came from. I knew that politics would be a very challenging career and that I would have to be very effective in my dealings with people. To have a good insight into human behaviour would make me a more effective politician. I also knew that to be a successful politician I would have to be able to speak well in public. When I had developed a good insight into human behaviour and a lot of experience as a public speaker, I decided to get involved in communications training.

Ireland changed a lot in the 1960s. Before then it was a small, backward country. The major changes were the introduction of Telefís Éireann, as it was then known, Vatican II, the economic development of the Lemass-Whittaker years, free education, and radio and television programmes which discussed issues that had never been discussed before. Many people used to attend meetings and they wanted to stand up and speak. However, most people find speaking in public very difficult. In 1971 I set up my first public speaking course. The aim of the course was to develop people's skills in public speaking, and to increase their confidence. This aim was achieved.

In 1972 Ireland voted to join what was then called the "Common Market", now the European Union. In those days the Irish economy was relatively unsophisticated and many organisations campaigned to vote against entry. It was outlined that the country could not compete with the other very advanced nations of Europe. Also, the women's movement was working hard for equality and to upgrade the role of women in their careers. There was opposition to this too. I was very committed to both assisting Irish people to cope with their more challenging lives and to helping women become more advanced and successful. I set up my communications skills course in March 1972 to achieve that.

The course covered the following areas:

· public speaking
· how to communicate effectively
· how to chair and attend meetings
· how to remember people's names
· how to think clearly under pressure
· how to eliminate doubts and negative thoughts

All of these topics helped to make the people who attended the course more self-confident.

In January 1973 a young man who was on one of my courses asked me whether I would be able to give advice on dealing with a friend of his who was very aggressive. This question was followed by one from a girl who told me that her boss was very arrogant and that she found it difficult to work with him. A few other people raised matters that concerned them about dealing with people.

I told them that I would discuss the issue the following week. Due to my knowledge of psychology and its obvious importance in this area I decided to upgrade the course to include a session on human behaviour.

In May 1973 a man asked for my opinion on conversation skills. He told me that he had attended a wedding the previous Saturday and that he was enjoying talking to many of his friends. The meal then started and he was put beside a few people whom he did not know and he found it very difficult to converse with them. Some were older than he was and they all knew each other. He thought that I might have some ideas on how to be a good conversationalist because he regarded me as a good speaker. In those days I had not given any thought to conversation skills due to the fact that I had a lot of friends and we got on well together. I had taken part in a conversation situation in 1967 which will be outlined in the chapter on conversation skills. When that question was put to me, other people in the class told me that they had difficulties conversing with people and that they would like to become better conversationalists.

I told the group that I would give the matter some thought and that I would discuss it with them at the next session. I spent a lot of time over the week thinking about how one could become a good conversationalist and decided to get the group to practice what I thought might work. When the next session started, I spent a half-hour discussing what might contribute to people becoming good conversationalists. I asked them to use what I had suggested and to give me a report at the next session. I continued preparing "How to Become a Good Conversationalist". I then started a role-play session and each participant conversed with me. Most of the ideas that I had devised worked very well. I was aware that many people would like to become better at conversations so I decided to include conversation skills on my course. It got a very good reaction from the participants.

The session on "Decision Making and Problem Solving" was included after I devised a system on how to make decisions and solve problems in 1974 when I went through a major crisis in my business. The Decision-Making and Problem Solving chapter will outline the key features of this part of the course.

The majority of people who came on my course from 1976 to the early 1980s did so to become more confident and better communicators. In the 1980s Ireland went through a serious economic crisis. In all the recessions of the past it was so-called "working-class" people who lost their jobs. In the recession of the 1980s all types of people suffered. Business and professional people went through the same crisis as tradespeople and unskilled workers. By the end of the 1980s people from all walks of life came on my course in order to upgrade their skills so that they could cope better if difficult situations were to arise. This persuaded me to make changes to my course and I included presentation skills, negotiation skills, and conflict resolution skills.

All of the sections in my course are covered in this book and I will not be just giving my opinions on what I think should be done in the areas that are covered. Everything that you will read will be of benefit to you. Thousands of people have improved their lives having taken part in my course over the past twenty-five years. However, to become a very self-confident person and an expert communicator it will be necessary to take part in a course which is participative: with each participant heavily involved in every session, rather than simply listening to the trainer talking. When I conduct my course I don't just give the information. I make the sessions interesting for the participants by doing my presentation of the course content with humour. I have written each chapter of this book in the same style as I give my course. The material is concise and easily accessible. While it is far more than a funny book it should be easy for you to read. I accept that some people may not agree with some of the things that I have written. It is also possible that some people who will review this book will give a negative reaction. I will not take that personally due to the fact that I am not just writing what I feel or think. The fact that my course has existed for 25 years and that most government departments, leading national and international companies and professional organisations constantly use my services is the reason why what is outlined works in practice.

On 2 February 1996 and on 16 April 1997, the Labour Party leader, Mr. Ruairi Quinn, T.D., then Minister for Finance, made an outstanding speech complimenting me for the contribution that I have made to assisting the people of Ireland. Over 30,000 Irish people have benefited greatly from the courses that I have conducted. This fact, and the comments from Mr. Ruairi Quinn would not have been possible if what I have devised and written did not work.

2

The Importance of
Communication Skills

The public image of a good communicator is a good speaker. There are many people who are very articulate with a good command of language, yet they are not very good communicators. Effective communication is more than just talking and conveying information. It is dealing with people in an effective way. All human beings are communicators. All human beings have to try to express their ideas and communicate with others. Some do it very well, while some don't do it very well.

The big advantage that a good speaker has is that they are given credit for abilities beyond those which they possess. The fact that they speak well impresses many people especially those who know that they lack similar speaking skills. While it is right to be impressed with the way people talk, it is the content of what they say that is more important. In the chapters on Human Behaviour, Negotiations, Conflict Resolutions and Meetings, the method of dealing with people, influencing and persuading them and sorting out problems, will be covered in detail.

This chapter outlines the central importance of communication skills. The ability to speak fluently and to convey information without ambiguity or misinterpretation is the major asset of a good communicator. The public in general are influenced in their thinking by people who speak well. In the past the people who influenced the thinking of the world were philosophers, poets, writers and theologians. They were individuals of considerable intellectual stature who wrote books which were read by well educated people. Their ideas were permeated down through the churches, universities and colleges. In today's world, the people who have the greatest influence tend to be politicians, people in the world of entertainment, broadcasters, journalists and the media in general. While some of these people are highly intelligent and deep thinking individuals, there are those who are what I would call lightweight populists. However, because they possess very good speaking skills, or because they are popular and well-known, they can have a lot of influence on people who read their articles, or listen to or watch their broadcasts. As I have outlined, a person who is a good speaker or has a lively personality will impress many people with their ideas. It is also true that well-known people can impress a lot of individuals. The fact that they are well-known can persuade some people that they are specialists in everything that they speak about.

For many years in the past, the individuals who had the most influence on people in Ireland were Catholic priests. They were of course specialists in theology and religious matters. If a priest gave his opinion on any other issue such as education, sport, music, theatre, films, etc., the majority of people would have accepted what his views were and not the views of the experts in those areas. In the 1960s major changes came to Ireland and the development of the media contributed to the fact that different types of people became more influential. Because some people became well-known and popular, the views that they expressed had a strong influence on some members of the public. Although I admire and respect some well-known people, I don't see them as experts on everything. A journalist, broadcaster, actor, musician or sportsperson will be very knowledgeable in the areas that they are involved in and I am willing to accept what they say in their areas of expertise. However, their views on all other matters are purely personal and while I might agree with some of the things that they say, I am not willing to accept all of their ideas just because they are well known, popular or have strong or likeable personalities or good speaking skills. Remember, it is the content of what people say that is important.

This is where a person's presentation skills can give them an advantage. Imagine watching a television programme where an issue is being discussed. The individual in favour of the topic is very intelligent and is clearly a deep thinker. However, he or she does not possess good communication or presentation skills, and speaks in a low, hesitant way. Many of the people who are listening will lose interest in what this person is saying. The individual who is opposing the issue could be a lightweight populist with a limited mind. However, because he or she has a good command of language and speaks very well, the viewers will find them more interesting and their views on the issue will influence more people. In this context presentation is more important than content. Many years ago politicians stood up on platforms outside churches or in town squares and addressed the public on their policies.

Their style of delivery, i.e., "presentation", did not matter a great deal. Now it is the complete opposite. The presentation of ideas is often more important than the content.

While presentation is important, it is essential that one should not allow it to influence one's thoughts. Presentation of ideas is like the presentation of products that people buy. A second rate product that is very well "presented", with the right name, size and colour, and which is promoted by good advertising, will walk off the shelves in stores. A first rate product badly "presented", with the wrong name, size and colour and the wrong packaging, will lie on the shelves indefinitely. In time, the second rate product may be exposed and the good one may have its day. But it is the "presentation" of the product that is frequently more important than its quality. It is the same with ideas. A bad idea which is well presented can impress and influence some people more than a good idea which is badly presented.

When people read an article in a newspaper, watch a person speak on a television programme or listen to them on the radio, it is important not to let their "presentation" have too much influence. The best thing to do is to try to get behind the "facade" and examine the "content" of what is being said. This is my opinion and one reason why "critics" are necessary.

If critics did not exist, then many people would succeed in doing ineffective things. For example, suppose critics did not exist and I became a pianist without any professional training. I would not be a good pianist. However, if I produced a CD and it was very well promoted the advertisement could say that I was an excellent pianist. People without much knowledge of classical music could be taken in by the advertising 'hype'. Due to the fact that critics exist, however, I would be evaluated and my weaknesses exposed.

While some critics are not very popular and may not be very good as critics, there is a need for them, I believe, in order to raise and maintain standards.

In this opening chapter I have outlined that good communication skills are very important and that good presentation skills give people an advantage. However, please bear in mind that it is very important not to be too impressed by people who are simply good speakers.

The following chapters will outline how good speaking skills can be linked with other skills in order to make people effective "communicators".

3
Self-Confidence

The public image of a confident person is an extrovert, the life and soul of the party, someone who always looks relaxed and at ease. This is not necessarily the case. There are many people who may be very outgoing but who lack faith in themselves and there are others who may be reserved or introverted but are very self-confident. Many people who have taken my course have told me that their friends thought that they were very confident because they were extroverts but that they themselves did not feel very assured. My definition of self-confidence is having a strong belief in oneself, and knowing and accepting one's abilities and limitations.

One of the main reasons why some people do not have a lot of self-confidence is that confidence and a strong sense of self-belief was not instilled into them when they were growing up. For generations there was the notion that confidence was equated with pride and pride was one of the seven deadly sins, the sin of Satan. If someone really believed in themselves and came across as very confident, they would have been regarded as being *full of themselves*.

"He has got a good opinion of himself"
"Who does she think she is"

These would have been the reaction to someone who spoke with confidence or who claimed to possess skills or abilities.

While boasting and bragging is not recommended and can come across as pretentious, it is good that people can accept their positive attributes. However, humility is important. My definition of humility is being able to admit mistakes, and to accept rejection or defeat, without feeling that one is useless. When I was growing up in the 1950s there was a view that children should be seen but not heard, that self-praise was no praise, and that pride must have a fall, speak when you are spoken to. While these attitudes no longer seem to exist, there are still some people who are being brought up without self-confidence being instilled into them.

When children are being brought up, there are many influences in their lives. In Ireland, the first and perhaps greatest influence would be religion. The importance of accepting the beliefs and values of the church to which they belong would be stressed. Parents, schools and the churches would convey this. The second major influence is education. The importance of becoming well educated is instilled into young people. All of us will remember when we were young and there were days when we did not want to go to school and how our parents sent us in, emphasising how important it was to be educated. As young people grow up, many of their parents will stress the importance of morality. There would be people who would have the value of good manners, politeness, eating habits, hygiene etc. instilled into them.

The one thing that many people do not have instilled into them however is self-confidence and a belief in themselves. It could be that their parents were lacking in confidence so they could not bring up their children to be confident. In the world in which we live, self-confidence is essential if we are to succeed and achieve our goals. The following story on how I developed my self-confidence is an instructive one.

When I was young in the 1950s and 1960s I had no confidence whatsoever. I was small, I had a stammer and I was a slow learner. I was shy and felt inferior to most other young people. After I made my First Communion I left the convent school and was put into a local national school. I was put back a year and served a second year in first class. That led to me being the oldest boy in the class and I was very self-conscious about that. It seemed to me that all the other boys were very intelligent and I would never put my hand up to answer a question, as I was terrified that I would say the wrong thing. There were some boys who looked very confident and who were always able to give the right answer.

There were exams every year at Christmas and in the summer. I failed the exams for some years, which devastated me. While I had a very good family and some very good friends, my days at school were very hard due to my lack of belief in myself. I saw myself as the smallest, least intelligent and least successful pupil. At sport I was a disaster. In the school that I was in students were sent to the Phoenix Park on Thursday afternoons to play football. I did not attend very often. On one occasion I was ordered to go. I was put in goal and let every goal in and in desperation I was taken out and put in the forwards. I then committed the coup de grace by scoring an own goal. To go into school on the next morning was a dreadful experience. From time to time, we had debates in school and I was always scared of being asked to take part. Even though I did not want to be asked I still envied the boys who could stand up and speak confidently. When I got into my teens, things became more difficult as I found it difficult to take full advantage of the opportunities opening up for teenagers at that time.

As I came near the end of my school period I did not know what I would do. For many years I thought that I would be a chemist like my father. One evening a group of us went into a pub and were discussing what we would like to do after we left school that summer. One boy said that he would like to be a solicitor, another would be joining the army, another wanted to be an architect, another a civil servant. I sat uncomfortably as I did not know what I wanted to do. I had planned to go into politics due to the background that I came from but I knew that I would have to find a "real career" before I could go into politics. I always had an interest in dealing with people and in human behaviour, so I decided to study psychology to see if my ideas about people and the way they should be treated were correct. I knew that politics would be very challenging and I wanted to be successful in that area, and felt that psychology would be useful in that context as well.

In the 1960s Ireland was going through great changes due to the introduction of Telefis Eireann (as it was then known), the Second Vatican Council and the development of the economy. There were many debating societies, debating the issues that were taking place. I was very interested in the changes and I attended a lot of the debates. However, due to my lack of confidence I was afraid to stand up and ask questions or make a statement and I envied the people who spoke so well and wished that I was like them. I used to attend a debate on a Saturday evening and the chairman had a system of getting the audience involved. Before the debate started, members of the audience who wished to make a comment, when the speakers on the panel had finished, could sign their name on a form on the chairman's desk.

One night there was a debate on the issue of the Irish language. In those days the Irish language was compulsory. A student could get honours in all other subjects but if they failed Irish they would not be awarded their Leaving Certificate. An organisation called "The Language Freedom Movement" was set up to oppose that. While I was in favour of the Irish language due to my strong nationalist background and my education in Colaiste Mhuire, I was opposed to the law as it then existed. I arrived at the hotel at seven o'clock on the Saturday night, an hour before the debate started and the room was empty. Because I felt strongly about the issue I put my name on the list of audience speakers. When the debate started the room was full with about a hundred people in attendance. I took a seat at the back of the room and when the debate ended the chairman started to call members of the audience. I was the third person to be called and I stood up and kept my hands on the chair in front of me and in my quiet voice said a few words about what I thought on the issue of keeping compulsory Irish. I felt very nervous but because I was at the back of the room I was able to say a few words. After less than a half a minute, I ended and the next person was called.

When I walked home that night I felt very well as I had done something that I always wanted to do but had previously been afraid to. The next week I went back and asked a question on the issue that was debated and for the following few weeks I got more involved by asking questions and giving my views on the issues. I then felt that I would like to go on to a debating panel. I approached the chairman and asked him if I could take part in a debate. He informed me that there would be a debate the following week on the issue of the building changes that were taking place in Dublin. The motion would be "That Dublin Town Should Come Tumbling Down". He had received a message from the person who was to oppose the motion that they would not be able to attend and he asked me would I be willing to oppose the motion. I agreed just because I wanted to take part in a debate. He introduced me to another speaker who would be on the same side as me. We met for a few nights and prepared and I was to be the first speaker on the opposition side.

When I arrived at Buswell's Hotel, I was quite nervous even though I was well prepared. A hundred and four people attended and after the chairman did his introduction, he called on the proposer to open the debate. He was excellent, a very good speaker, very confident and had a great sense of humour. He was urbane, witty, scathing. The audience were very impressed and were laughing, applauding and enjoying what he was saying. I felt very uncomfortable as I knew that I could not be as good as him. He ended his delivery, sat down and got a great reaction from the audience. The chairman then introduced me. I lost the power of my voice and my body and could not stand up. The chairman said "Are you going to speak?" I replied in a low voice "No, I can't." The chairman then said to the audience "Ladies and gentlemen, I will see if I can get this chap to speak." He then said to me "Frank, just stay seated and read what you have written." I started to read slowly then my colleague gave me a dig with his elbow and I stood up leaning on the table and in a low and slow voice read what I had written on the subject. Most of the audience could not hear me and after only one minute I sat down. The reaction that I got was not good. The vote was then taken and the proposer got one hundred and two votes and I got just two votes from two friends. He won by a landslide.

I went home that night shattered. My low confidence and lack of self esteem dominated me. I decided that I would never take part in a debate again. A week later it dawned on me that I wanted to go into politics and to do that I would have to be able to speak in public. I did not know what to do. It then struck me that the reason why I did so badly was that the proposer was so experienced as a public speaker. He was also ten years older than me. I thought that if I was debating against someone who was similar to me in both age and experience I might do better. I decided to try it once more and I applied again for a panel discussing an issue that I was interested in.

The debate was on the issue of "The Effects That Telefis Eireann Have Had On Ireland". I wanted to propose the motion outlining how it was improving the country and I was selected. My opponent was a young girl who was conservative and opposed to many of the programmes. She spoke well on the issue and won the debate by only two votes. I felt that I had done well losing by only two votes.

The next debate that I took part in was proposing the motion "That The United States Has Forfeited Its Claim To The Statue of Liberty". While I had nothing against America or the American people, I was opposed to the Vietnam War which was a major issue in those years, and I gave a very good speech and won the debate. For the next few months I took part in a lot of debates and while I did not win them all I did very well and my voice improved a lot and I became very confident by standing up and speaking in front of large groups of people.

To be able to stand up and speak in front of a group is one of the most effective ways to build one's confidence. There have always been good debating societies in the universities and the students who have taken part in the debates had tended to become very confident and have done very well in their careers when they left the university. I got a lot of people on my course in public speaking who had been to university. However, they had been too frightened to take part in debates.

In the parish that I was in I got involved in an organisation and spent a lot of time debating, speaking in public and attending meetings. That contributed to me developing a lot of confidence. I then started doing a course in public speaking and debating for young people. When I saw that many people were interested in learning to debate and speak in public I decided to go into that area as a career. What contributed to my self-confidence was seeing myself standing up and speaking, thinking on my feet. Whenever I had a challenging situation I would stop and say to myself "If I can stand up and speak before a group on something that I don't believe in, then what is stopping me from doing this?" In some debates I did speak on things that I did not agree with which is part of the process of debating.

The best way for a person to develop self-confidence is to accept themselves as they are and to dedicate themselves to improving their abilities and overcoming their limitations. While all human beings have both positive and negative attributes no one selects them. They are part of their lives. For example, I did not choose to be born. I did not choose to be born on the island of Ireland, in the city of Dublin, into the religious and social background that I was in. I did not choose to be male, heterosexual, or to stop growing at five feet, five inches. I did not select any of my abilities or shortcomings. The reason why I lacked self-confidence years ago was due to the concern that I had about my shortcomings. I felt very bad about being small, about being a slow learner, about being ineffective in sport and having a stammer.

Lots of other people that I knew were taller than me, good-looking, they spoke well, they were good students and they were better than me at sport. I felt very unconfident. When I got into my teens I was afraid of going to a disco and asking a girl to dance. I was twenty-two when I had my first date. I would recommend that one should accept what I have outlined about not being put off or discouraged by one's supposed shortcomings. As I have said we do not select either our positive or negative attributes. The way to develop self-confidence is to accept oneself as one is and to both upgrade one's abilities and eliminate one's shortcomings where possible.

Since the spring of 1969 I have been very self-confident. I have total faith in myself. I have no doubts about my abilities and I accept the human shortcomings that I have. I could not increase my height, but I do not feel unconfident about not being tall. My stammer went, my confidence developed. I have made mistakes and have had bad problems but I can cope with anything that happens due to my total faith in myself. In the course that I devised I encouraged participants to do what I have done and vast numbers of people have increased their confidence as a result.

While one should admire other people for the abilities that they have, one should never compare oneself with them and expect to be like them. If one has a problem or a lack of ability it is essential to take responsibility for it and if it is possible to overcome it, then that should be done. One thing that influences the confidence of people is the thoughts that come into their minds. If the thoughts are positive then the individual will be more at ease and more confident. However, if the thoughts are negative then that can undermine confidence. A positive mental attitude is essential for one to be confident.

While there is no way of transforming a person into a perfect human being with no shortcomings or problems people can become very confident by learning to accept themselves as they are. When people leave my course at the end of the programme they do not walk out as superman or superwoman. However, they do leave feeling a lot more confident.

4

Conversation Skills

Starting conversations can be difficult for some people and this chapter will define the attributes of the good conversationalist and how to develop them.

There are six main stages in being a good conversationalist.

1. Being a good listener

It is very important to be a good listener. There are some reasons why people don't listen well. It may be that they have no interest in the topic that is being discussed. The person who is talking can cause people to "switch-off." If the speaker has a low, boring, monotone voice, it will not be easy for someone to pay attention and be interested in what is being said.

When a person is speaking to an individual, in conversation, discussing an issue at a meeting or around a dinner table or standing up in front of a group and making a presentation, it is essential that they speak in a lively way. This will hold the interest of the listeners and convey the information without ambiguity or misinterpretation. In the past I knew a man that I used to meet on the street in Dublin and although he was very intelligent, well-educated, widely read and extensively travelled he was what I called "The greatest bore west of Suez." Sometimes when I saw him walking up the street I would try to avoid him. As I used to jokingly say, "He puts years on me and I can't afford that." His voice was very low and monotone and he was very repetitive. Many other people that I knew also found it difficult to listen to him. It was unfortunate because he had a lot of interesting thoughts. If his delivery had been livelier he would have been a very interesting conversationalist.

If a person went to a party and was introduced to me and I began telling them about a book that I had read, a film that I had seen, or a concert that I had attended and I spoke in a low, monotone voice, they would not find me interesting. Out of courtesy they might stay and listen for a while. If someone else asked them "What were you talking to that fellow about?" they could honestly say "I have no idea, he was meandering on about a concert that he attended, I was bored listening to him." That would have been my fault, as I would have failed to hold their attention and would have been responsible for them not listening.

Another reason why people don't listen is that they are thinking ahead to what they are going to say next. This occurs when a controversial issue is being discussed and if people hold different views, they will tend to be formulating their responses rather than listening to what is being said. The hotter the issue becomes, the more likely it is that people will not listen to the arguments of their opponents and it is usual to find some people interrupting the speaker in order to counter their argument. This leads to people talking *at* rather than *to* each other.

2. Being well-informed

The second attribute of the good conversationalist is being well-informed and having a good general knowledge so that they can speak to any type of person in a relaxed manner regardless of what they may have in common.

While most people are well-informed on all the issues that get lots of publicity they will not be knowledgeable on everything. It is easy to converse with people who share their interests. However, when they encounter people with different interests, they can find it difficult to keep a conversation going. For example, assume there is a man called John who is well-educated, reads good quality newspapers, takes an interest in politics, the European Union, world issues, theatre and supports the arts. When he meets other people who have those interests, he can talk knowledgeably, at length and without difficulty.

One day he attends a wedding and having spent time talking to friends and acquaintances, he is placed at a table beside Frank. Frank is a totally different type of person. He reads tabloids, watches game shows, chat shows, quizzes and soaps on television and is heavily into the lighter things in life. They have little in common and the conversation can be difficult for both of them. While most people have friends who are similar to themselves in age, background, income level and who share common interests, they can from time to time meet up with people with whom they have little in common and it is essential that they can converse without pressure. There was a time when people mixed only with others of a similar background but in this more egalitarian age, there are opportunities for all kinds of people to meet each other if only for a short time at a function or attending an event. The ability to be able to meet with anyone in a relaxed manner and converse at ease is a skill worth possessing.

The best way to develop this ability is to follow what is happening in current affairs in general, even in areas in which one has no particular interest. When I was young I was very small and that led to me not being able to play sport. I lost interest in sport and spent my spare time reading and writing poetry. In those years I was not a specialist in communication skills and I did not know how to converse with people who were very interested in sport. Many years later I decided that I wanted to have more friends and I knew that they would not be just interested in the things that I liked. I knew that many people would be very interested in sport so I took an interest in it. I could not play it but I started watching major events on television. When I met with people who were interested in sport I told them that I did not know much about it and asked them to inform me about what had happened or could happen in particular sporting events. I always showed that I was interested in what they were talking about.

When television started in Ireland in the 1960s I watched a lot of it and found it very interesting for a long time. However, now that I have to work long hours I do not have the time to watch it as much as I used to. I fully appreciate that most people are interested in television and radio programmes and when I meet with people who are, I am willing to show an interest in what they are interested in. It would be easy to live in a cocoon, taking an interest only in the aspects of life to which one is committed and ignoring everything else. A person doing that would only be able to converse with people like themselves. It is better to be able to meet with all kinds of people and converse with them in a relaxed, informed and easy way.

This raises the question as to where people can get the information that they require. As we know it comes from a wide range of sources, including newspapers, radio, television, books, magazines and other people. It is essential that people's minds are open to ideas from all sources. However, it is also important that the views that they hold have been thought through so that they can defend the issues that they support. A person can *feel* strongly about something without ever having really *thought* about it. Because they have an emotional commitment to it they accept it as their view. When the issue comes up in a conversation or discussion, they speak up and say "I'm against that" or "I'm in favour of this." It is what they *feel* not what they *think*. Having then committed themselves to that view, they are reluctant to back down and admit that they may have been wrong so they defend what they have said.

In order to be able to meet with all types of people and to converse with them in a relaxed and easy way, making an effort to be well-informed on as many issues as possible is essential. I appreciate that some people will not be interested in doing this as it can be challenging for them. For a person who is not interested in classical music or opera they can find it difficult to read about it or listen to items about it. If a person is not interested in something they can not be expected to be able to talk about it with the same knowledge or enthusiasm as those who are committed to it. They should, however, be able to show an interest in the subject and to ask relevant and interesting questions. If a person wishes to be able to attend any event in a relaxed and easy way and to converse with any type of individual that they will meet, doing what I have suggested will benefit them.

3. Being at ease when meeting people for the first time

From time to time, people may have to go to a function on their own, at which they don't know the other guests and they may have to meet and converse with strangers. Many people find this difficult and are reluctant to walk up to someone, introduce themselves and initiate a conversation. Some people will stand alone and hope that another individual will approach them. However, that is unlikely to happen too often. If the person who walks into a room at a gathering is well-known, a celebrity or a public figure, then it might happen due to the fact that some people like to meet well-known or distinguished human beings.

The reason why many people are reluctant to approach other people is that they have an underlying fear of rejection. Most people don't like being rejected and may take it personally, especially if they are not very confident. I do not recommend walking up to a group of people who are talking among themselves and expect to be invited to join their company. That group may be discussing personal matters, talking "shop" or just enjoying each other's company. The ideal thing to do is to look for someone who is also on their own, go up to them, introduce oneself and start a conversation. This may seem easier said than done, due to the fact that the person approached may not want to talk to the person that they have just met. It is essential not to take that personally and feel upset. If I approached someone and they did not show an interest in me, left me quickly and greeted someone else I would not feel sad. As I have said for many years to my students "I am not running a fan club." I don't expect everybody to like me. The law of averages says that a proportion of people that I meet won't like me or may find me uninteresting. When I was very young I would have been upset if that happened but since I developed my self-confidence I have been able to accept rejection.

When some people go through a challenging situation they will resort to alcohol to assist them. While a drink can be very pleasant when we are relaxed and at ease, it is not a good idea to rely on it to cope with a difficulty.

4. Starting conversations

The state of the weather is perhaps the most popular opening for many people. Lots of people refer to it even though they may prefer to be a little more original. However, it does start the ball rolling as many people find it difficult at times to initiate conversations.

Conversations amongst strangers, or people who do not know each other very well, will have to start with "small talk." It would be strange for a person to introduce himself or herself and launch into a conversation on a serious matter. For example, I am unlikely to meet a person and shake hands with them and say "Hello, my name is Frank, tell me are you in favour of euthanasia?" While we could at a later stage discuss that issue to start the conversation with it would be crazy.

"Small talk" could include questions like, "Are you a friend of Martina?" Martina being the hostess of the party. "Do you know many people here?," "Isn't this a lovely building?," "Aren't those pictures lovely?" If it is during the summer one could ask "Have you had your holidays yet?" If it is during the time of a major event, a big sports occasion, the Eurovision song contest, an election, or a major public controversy then it would be easy enough to raise the matter early in the conversation. The state of the weather is the most popular opening, as both sides will always agree on what is said.

After the small talk is over it is necessary to develop the conversation and one of the best ways to get a conversation going is to talk to people about their favourite topic. How does one know what an individual's favourite topic is? Is it sport, theatre, music, television? The answer is simple. For *most* people their favourite topic is *themselves*. Many years ago I read a biography of Benjamin Disraeli, who was Prime

Minister of Great Britain in the last century, who said "Talk to a person about themselves and they will listen for hours." He was right. Most people like to talk about themselves. Things they have done, places that they visited, interesting people that they have met, victories achieved, good things. While most people don't like boasting and bragging they would still like other people to know about their achievements and interests. The good conversationalist encourages people to open up and talk about themselves.

This, however, raises the question "Are there some questions that should not be asked?" The answer is: "Of course - it is not right to ask *personal questions*." But what is a personal question? What is personal to one person will not be to another.

There are some individuals who are prepared to tell people what political party they support, whereas others would regard that as a *personal* matter. Most people would avoid asking questions relating to a person's personal life, their age, their income or about their illnesses or family problems.

There are some seemingly harmless questions that people ask that can sometimes elicit a negative response. One of these is a question that many people ask, "What do you do for a living?" While it seems a harmless question some people can react negatively to it. In the 1980s when Ireland was going through an economic crisis many people lost their jobs. I spent a good deal of my time conducting my courses for ANCO (now FÁS) for unemployed people. Many of them told me how difficult it was for them to have to say to people in a group that they were unemployed. Even though it was not their fault that they were made redundant, they felt very upset having to say that they were unemployed. For people who have never experienced unemployment, it may not be something that they are aware of. It is better to let a person say what they do for a living and to show an interest in their job, their company or industry. While there are some people who don't find it difficult to admit that they do not have a job, it is better to let them raise the issue.

Another reason why some people may not like to discuss their work is that they may feel that their job is not as prestigious as the positions of those surrounding them. While some people would believe that all jobs are good and it is wrong to grade them or regard them as basic, the reality is that many societies do tend to categorise jobs.

Many people have told me that they felt uncomfortable in groups where people were discussing their work and they believed that their jobs were less important or skilful. If a person goes to a business function where all those attending are from different companies, then it is all right to ask people where they work or what they do. However, at a social event where there is a mixture of people it is better to let the other person raise the issue and then talk to them about their job.

Another challenging question to ask would be "Where do you live?" If someone lives in an area that has a bad reputation for crime, drugs or social deprivation, then it might be very difficult for them to have to announce it, especially if they are in the company of people who in their opinion live in "good areas." Over the years I have met many people who told me how difficult it was for them to admit where they lived. To those who come from the better parts of cities or towns, it may not be an issue of any importance, but it can be to others. Once again, there are exceptions to the rule and there are people who don't feel bad about where they live and they are very pleased to live there. However, when people first meet it is not possible to know their feelings on this issue so it is safer not to raise it.

A third seemingly harmless question would be to ask a married couple if they have children. Back in 1968 I was doing one of my first jobs in market research and called to a married couple who were in their mid-thirties in Rathfarnham. I was given a sheet of paper with a number of questions and I was told to get answers for them all. After I asked them if they came from Ireland, if they travelled to work by car or public transport, if they took a foreign holiday and some other questions I then asked them "Do you have any children?" They both looked at each other, seemed to frown and in a quiet voice said "No." The lady looked very upset. I then realised what I had done. Here were two people who would have liked to have had a family but for some reason they could not. I had upset them. I did not intend to do that but I was told to ask them that question and in those days I was not as experienced in dealing with people. Also I came from a family with seven children. While there are some married people who do not have a family and who may not have any difficulty talking about it, there are others for whom it is a major aspect of their lives.

Therefore it is better to let people raise matters of a potentially sensitive nature themselves and if they wish to discuss them to show an interest in what they are saying.

The best way to get a conversation going would be to talk to people about their hobbies, interests, holidays and matters that can not cause them to react negatively.

In September 1967 I learned an invaluable lesson in how to get a conversation started and keep it going. I went with a friend of mine to a house out in Rush in North County Dublin and was introduced to the man of the house and his daughter. After a few minutes of small talk between the four of us, my friend went off with the young woman to another room and I was left with her father in the drawing room. He seemed a quiet sort of person who did not have much to say and I was also not a very good communicator. I can recall the conversation, it went something like this.

"That was very bad weather we had these last few days."

"Yes, but the forecast is good for the weekend."

Silence.

I did not know what to say next and he seemed to be having a similar difficulty. I began to feel very uncomfortable and kept thinking, "What will I say next?" but could not come up with anything. I heard a dog bark in the garden and I looked out of the window. I saw a beautiful garden, covered with lovely flowers and plants. I said to the man:

"That is a beautiful garden that you have, those flowers are lovely."

"Do you like flowers, Frank?" he said, "Are you keen on gardening?"

"I do love flowers but I am not any good at dealing with them," I said.

"Would you like to come out and I will show you around," he said.

"Oh yes," I said.

Anything to get out of the room.

He brought me into the garden which was very big and for almost an hour he showed me the different flowers, plants and trees. He did all the talking and he was very knowledgeable about his great interest. All I did was to ask a few simple questions such as:

"What is that?"

"How do you maintain those?"

"Do they last during the winter?"

He gave me a lot of information and I learned a lot about the things that he was very interested in. When we came to the last section he said to me, "I hope you found this interesting."

"Oh yes," I replied, "you really are an expert on gardening." He smiled and said, "Well, it is my great passion in life."

We then went back into the house and were joined by his daughter and my friend and we all had some tea. As I was leaving the house he came up and said to me "You must come back and see me again Frank,

I found you a very interesting conversationalist."

As I was driving home I was amazed at what he had said about me being an interesting conversationalist. I had said very little. Four years later it dawned on me. (As you can see I was slow on the uptake.) I had listened to that man. I had made him feel important. He had an audience of **one** and in a nice manner he was able to **show off** his superior knowledge in his area of interest. I never forgot that lesson and it has helped me to get conversations going ever since.

Many people are like that man. They love to impress other people with their interests, knowledge or achievements. While a lot of people don't like to boast or brag, they still get great satisfaction by being well-thought of by others. So one of the best ways to get a conversation going is to show a genuine interest in the other person and to encourage them to open up and talk about themselves.

Many people use clichés when they talk. As we know, lots of people say to individuals that they meet "How are you?" Let's say I know a woman called Mary and she is feeling very bad due to a health problem or a crisis that she is having. I meet her and I say "Hello, Mary. How are you?" Is she supposed to tell me a lie and say "I'm grand, fine?" When I meet people I don't ask them that question. I greet them by name and if it is some time since we last met I will say "I'm very pleased to meet you again." When we part company I won't order them to "take care." I just say goodbye. I have been told by people that they do not like being asked how they are when they are in bad form, even though they often say this to people. While I don't believe that most people are annoyed with being asked how they are or told to take care I do regard these phrases as "clichés."

Dealing With People Who Have Little To Say

While most people like to talk about themselves, there are those who are the exact opposite, who do not like talking about themselves.

There are many reasons for this. Some people prefer to keep to themselves and are reluctant to discuss matters with others. There are those who are quiet, private, introverted and even some who are unfriendly. They are, of course, entitled to be like this and if they are unwilling to respond to one's questions then there is nothing that can be done about it. It is essential not to blame oneself if the other person refuses to converse. If you were to meet me at a function, showed an interest in me and tried to generate a conversation, and I made no effort to respond, then it would be best for you not to say, "I could not talk to that man." It was not your problem, because I made no effort to contribute to the conversation.

Did you ever try playing a game of tennis on your own? You hit the ball over the net. Unless there is someone to hit it back then there is no game. Conversations are the same. It takes at least two people to get a conversation going.

There is, however, a reason why some people find it difficult to converse with others. Did it ever occur to you that someone might feel uncomfortable in your company? Most of us would regard ourselves as friendly people and would be a little upset if we were to hear that another person did not feel relaxed while with us. However, it is possible and it is no reflection on us. The following story will explain how this can happen.

Some years ago I was looking out of the window of my former training centre in Mespil Road and I saw a beautiful top of the range Mercedes slowing down across the road. The driver got out, walked across the road and came into my office. He was interested in taking part in my Communications Training Programme and I went through all of the aspects of the course with him. He felt that it would be helpful to him so he decided to join up. I gave him the application form and he took out his pen and cheque book and was about to start writing, when he stopped and asked me:

"What kind of people will be on this course?"

"Well," I said "the participants will range in age from early twenties to late fifties."

"I don't mean that," he said. "Will they all be well-educated people?"

"Yes, I replied "most of them will be."

"Will some of them have degrees?" he asked.

"Oh, yes, some of them will have," I said.

He put his pen down and said, "I don't think that I could join a course like that." I asked him why and he told me his life story.

He came from a small farm in Co. Leitrim and left school very early. After spending some time working on the land, he moved to England and got a job on a building site. He worked very hard and returned to Ireland in the late 1960s when the building boom was in progress. In the middle 1970s he set up his own building firm and became quite a wealthy man. However, he was very conscious of his lack of formal education and told me that he would be very uncomfortable in a course with well-educated people. He told me that when he went into his bank he felt uneasy talking to his manager, who spoke very well and was a well-educated man. I remember saying to him:

"I'm sure when your manager sees your account, he would not mind having some of your money."

"I would give a lot of my money to have some of his education," he replied.

I was concerned about his fear of joining a group of well-educated people so to assist him, I asked him to come to the first night of the course and if he decided that he did not want to do it then he could leave. He agreed and when he arrived I placed him beside a person who was closer to him in background and education and during the break he spoke to a few people and they let him do a lot of the talking about his job. He left the opening session quite relaxed and came back for the next session and stayed on the course. He developed a lot of confidence and at the end he was delighted that he had taken the course.

This was a man who felt very uncomfortable in the company of those who were more educated than himself. There are many people like him and I have met them during the years that I have been in the training area. That could be one reason why a person may find it difficult to take part in a conversation with other people.

I met another man who did my course back in 1979 and he told me why he felt uneasy in some people's company. He was 4'11" and was very conscious of the fact that he was small. He told me that he did not like going to receptions or parties where people stood talking, as he was the smallest in the group and those around him looked down at him. What they were doing was being polite and establishing eye contact with him but he saw it differently. Most people who are of average height or tall would be surprised to hear that someone thought they were looking down at them.

If a person speaks with an accent that is regarded as upper class, then others may feel uneasy in the company of that individual and become more conscious of their own accent and grammar. These are just some examples as to why someone may feel ill at ease with others.

Most people regard themselves as ordinary due to the fact that they are not well-known, or rich and do not have high-powered jobs. However, it is possible that other individuals could see them in a different way. Because some people may think that they have not achieved a lot in their lives, they can see other people who have been successful as superior to themselves. A very useful skill to possess is the ability to make everyone feel at ease with each other. Some people have this talent and it is a great asset as it means that one can meet with every type of person in a relaxed manner and talk to them.

5. Coping with lack of knowledge

All people are out of their depth on some issues. If they were to walk into the local library they would see great tomes all around the room on every subject from astrology to zoology. No matter how intelligent they may be or how long they live, they can only assimilate a minute proportion of all the knowledge in the world. As Plato, the great philosopher said, "The more I learn, the more aware of my ignorance I become." From time to time they may find themselves in a group where a topic of which they know nothing is being discussed. If all the other people are knowledgeable on the topic, then they could feel a little uneasy. A really confident person is one who can state openly, "I am out of my depth on this subject" or "I know absolutely nothing about this" and feel relaxed and at ease while saying it.

Unfortunately, there are some people who would feel very self-conscious and would be afraid to offer a view in case it sounded stupid to others. They may remain silent for quite some time and then they may think, "If I say something now, they will look at me anyway," so they say nothing.

In September 1992, we had a currency crisis and I found myself one night amongst a group of people from the financial world who were discussing the issue. One of the few things that I was aware of was that mortgages would go up and how it would affect business. The rest of the group were experts in the area of finance and they were discussing the subject in technical terms. I had to say, "I am out of my depth on this. Would you explain how this and that will affect so and so." I got a lot of interesting information, learned things that were new to me and became more knowledgeable about the aspects of currency. Even though I knew very little, I was still able to participate in the conversation and make a contribution to the discussion. Many years ago I would have stayed silent and felt uneasy. Now I am able to admit that I am out of my depth on many issues and make no apologies for it.

If people are not experienced in a particular area or lack knowledge on the matter that is being discussed, they should never try to bluff or apologise, but should just admit that they know little or nothing about the topic, and ask meaningful questions.

6. Feeling comfortable with and equal to all people

The final trait of the good conversationalist is having the ability to feel comfortable in the company of every person, no matter who they are. Many people feel at ease with those who are similar to themselves but if they meet someone who is well-known, distinguished, famous or very wealthy, they may feel uncomfortable in their company. It is my opinion that when we meet with people, we should see them as fellow members of the human race. We should never be in awe of a human being or feel inferior to them.

In the past, people were brought up to feel inferior to those who came from the higher social classes, who had titles or positions of importance. Thankfully, that has changed as many of the top people in most countries have come from ordinary backgrounds and have succeeded due to the more egalitarian and democratic societies that have developed over the years. However, there are still people who retain the attitude of subservience to those whom they consider to be above them. It is impossible to feel at ease in someone's company if we think that they are superior to us. Among the vast majority of civilised people, I do not believe that any one human being is superior to another **as an individual**. In specific areas people are, of course, more qualified or more skilful than others are. There are doctors, lawyers, teachers, business people and accountants who are more qualified and experienced than some of their competitors and one could say that they are **superior** in their particular area of expertise. But as **human beings**, they are not superior.

It is right that we should respect and admire people because of their achievements, talent, ability, the contributions that they have made to society or the important positions that they hold. If I were to meet a Head of State, a Government Minister, an Ambassador from another country, or a leading Churchman, I would give them the respect that their position is due. I would wait to be introduced to them, address them by their title and treat them with respect. But I would not feel in awe of them or be afraid to talk to them. While I would not be equal to them in terms of **position**, I would consider myself equal to them as a fellow member of the human race.

Over the years, I have sponsored a number of concerts by some of the world's leading artistes. After the concert, there would be a queue of people approaching them for their autographs. I have seen some of those people looking ill at ease and obviously in awe of the musician.

While I had the height of respect for their talent and admired them greatly, I still saw them as people, not as Gods. There are people who will disagree with me on this matter. There are those who like the idea of feeling **superior** to other human beings. For some, they like to feel "Socially Superior" and look down on those who come from what they consider a lower class background. Then there are those who like to feel "Intellectually Superior" and look down on those who are not gifted with their intelligence. Others like to feel "Racially Superior" and look down on people from a different race or colour. There are those who like to feel "Religiously Superior" and who regard their religion as superior to other religions. One of the reasons why so much conflict has existed in the history of the world is that leaders of one country did not see their neighbours as their equals but as inferior and, therefore, felt that they had to be invaded and their culture and way of life destroyed.

Some years ago a young man aged about 21 participated in my Communications Training Programme. He worked in a bank and shared the same floor as the Chief Executive. He told me that he was always uncomfortable when he saw the head of the bank, and that he would run into a side room if he noticed him coming along the corridor. After I covered the section on conversation skills, he started thinking about what I suggested.

At the end of my course I conduct an assessment at which each participant tells the group how they have used the skills and how they have benefited from the course. This young man stood up and told the group that one Monday morning he was in the lift and he heard someone approaching it. He put his finger on the hold button to make the lift available to the person, who happened to be the Chief Executive. He greeted the Chief Executive with a smile and asked him if he had a good weekend. The Chief Executive asked him his name, the department that he worked in and how long he had been in the bank. The young man told the class that he passes the Chief Executive several times a week and that while he addresses him formally and has great respect for him, he no longer sees him as a God but as a human being.

The six principles outlined in this chapter, if implemented, will increase everyone's ability to become a really good conversationalist.

1. Being a good listener.

2. Being well-informed about what is happening in the world even if one is not very interested in some aspects of it.

3. Being aware that some people can be uneasy when meeting new people.

4. Talking to people about themselves in a non-personal capacity and about their interests.

5. Admitting when one is out of one's depth.

6. Seeing every person that one meets as an equal member of the human race, whatever his or her status.

Good conversation skills make it a lot easier to go to parties, receptions or meetings on your own and converse with all types of people.

5

Human Behaviour

One of the greatest skills that a person can possess in life is the ability to get on well with people. To be able to approach individuals on sensitive or delicate issues, or to raise matters that might be critical of someone, without upsetting them is an admirable talent. To be able to win others around to one's point of view and get them to abandon what they have committed themselves to is equally useful, as is the ability to be able to influence and persuade people to accept one's ideas.

To achieve these things, it is necessary to have more than just a good command of language. It is essential to have an insight into human behaviour, how human beings think, act and react. A very important point to keep in mind is that the expression on one's face, one's tone of voice, choice of words and body language are factors that will determine to a considerable degree how what one says is received by others.

Another vital factor is an understanding of what motivates the human species. While the majority of people are capable of being very rational, reasonable and logical, the same individuals can be the total opposite on a specific issue or in a particular mood. The major factors that motivate people are pride, image, fear, jealousy, insecurity and ambition. The highly effective communicator is aware of these aspects and how they influence people's thoughts and reactions. This chapter will go through all these factors and will demonstrate how each one can influence human behaviour.

1. Pride

Pride is part of the human condition. Most people have an element of pride within them. Pride in their country, their county, their religion, their profession or trade and their family, to name the major ones. All of these are harmless. Pride becomes a problem when a person is unwilling to admit that they are wrong, that they have made a mistake, that they should have done something that they did not do or visa-versa.

It is essential to be aware that human beings can get very defensive when they are challenged on certain issues. The following areas are major sources of outrage to lots of people.

(a) Criticism

While many people are committed to criticising others, they are not capable of accepting criticism themselves. When an individual is criticised no matter how accurately, they can get angry, defensive and perhaps abusive to those who criticise them. They may defend what they have done, and justify and rationalise their actions, no matter how outrageous these actions have been. The main point to remember is that while the criticism was aimed at the action of the individual, it can be taken by the accused as a criticism of themselves. Many people take criticism personally.

The classic example would be two people discussing an issue. It is possible that one or both have never thought through the matter but have an emotional commitment to it. When the first person outlines their stance on the subject, the second one jumps in and expresses a contrary view. Both sides have now committed themselves to their respective positions and even if one of them begins to realise that they have been wrong, they will find it difficult to back down and admit it. If there is a group of people listening to the discussion that will make it even more difficult for the individual to admit their mistake.

(b) Telling people that they are wrong – pointing out their mistakes

Another area where pride arises is when someone is criticised for having done something or having made a mistake. Many people resent being told that they have done something wrong, even if there is plenty of evidence to prove it. They will feel that it is their duty to defend themselves at all costs and this leads to arguments with both sides talking **at** rather than **to** each other.

(c) Correcting People

Most people do not like to be corrected by others and tend to get defensive when it happens. When people were very young both their parents and schoolteachers had to correct them, tell them what to do and what not to do. While the children would not have liked that, they did accept it. Later when they grew up and went to work, their managers also corrected them and ordered them around, and the individual's reaction would be similar. However, people do not like to be corrected by friends, colleagues or individuals on the same level. The person who wants to correct someone should do so in a constructive way. Helping the individual to see their own mistakes and letting them admit their errors, is a very useful way to correct someone without antagonising them. Negative things to say would be "You did not handle that matter in the right way, you forgot to include...... in your decision, why don't you look at this in more detail?" This would be interpreted by the individual as a form of criticism and although they may not respond in an aggressive or negative way, they would be likely to feel upset and could develop a negative feeling towards the person who spoke to them in that way.

I am constantly approached by people in the training area requesting me to include them on my training panel. All the trainers that are on the panel now are very qualified and conduct the courses very well and this has been the case for many years. However, in my earlier days only private individuals came on my evening course. Companies did not tend to send people on courses. I did all the sessions except on a few occasions when I was ill and I used other trainers. While some of them were very good there were a few who were not. And I had to approach them on the matter.

In 1979 I got a dose of the flu and I could not attend my evening course in communication skills for a few weeks. I did not want to cancel the course as that would have caused a difficulty for the participants. A few weeks earlier I met a man who was a trainer in sales, customer care and time management. He convinced me that he could conduct training in communication skills. I got him to take over my course for three sessions. When I took over the last session I got a negative reaction from some of the people who felt that he was not a good communications trainer. As I was very committed to the highest standards on my course, I had to raise the matter with him.

I contacted him and asked him to meet me. I spent some time preparing for the meeting that I knew would be upsetting for him and difficult for me. I thought about his personality, temperament, and how he might react to being told that I would not use his services again. I was aware that there would be no easy way to tell him this and that while I had the right to take this decision, I did not want to send him out feeling that he was a failure. He was an intelligent and hard working person and I wanted him to leave my office in as positive a mood as possible under the circumstances. When he entered the office, I greeted him with a firm handshake and sat beside him rather than sitting behind my desk as I did not want to erect a barrier between us.

I started off in a friendly manner and asked him how he was getting on with his favourite hobby which was golf. We spoke for a few minutes about his progress in sport and I let him do a lot of the talking. I then decided to intervene and raise the matter. I started by thanking him for assisting me when I was sick and asked him to outline how he conducts the courses in Time Management, Sales and Customer Care. I complimented him on his knowledge of those courses and told him that I expected that the people who attended *his* courses would be very pleased. I did not flatter him but gave him appreciation. I then said, mentioning his name, "While you are very good in the areas that you specialise in, there are a few shortcomings that you have, just like me."

Because I established a good rapport with him, he did not feel too upset when I went through the issues that I raised. I did not criticise him or strongly outline what people had said about him. Instead I emphasised that the most important thing was that the participants on the course must be satisfied that they would get a lot from it and the losses that the company would experience if it got a negative reaction. I outlined to him mistakes that I had made in the past when I was less experienced and how I overcame them to the benefit of the business. This helped him to see what he had done wrong and how that had contributed to the negative reaction that I had received about him. I requested him to spend some time upgrading his skills and to come back to me when he was satisfied that he had done so.

When he left the office, he did so in a good mood. He was upset that he had caused me a problem but he did not leave angry with me and this is because I dealt with the issue in a constructive way.

It is never easy to criticise people but if one prepares for the meeting and treats the individual in a positive way, then it is easier to get them to accept that they have done something wrong. Another area where criticism can make people very angry is when their ideals, beliefs or views are opposed or rejected by others. As was mentioned earlier, many people take things personally.

For example, while the majority of people in a country are very committed to their country, its traditions, culture and achievements, they are willing to accept whatever shortcomings it may have. Some people will be willing to admit that to others. However, if a foreigner was to outline these same shortcomings many people would take it personally and become very upset and annoyed. They would feel that it was their duty to defend their country and its culture.

Within countries there are many counties and regions and lots of people are very committed to their county. If a citizen from one county was to criticise another county the individual from the county that was criticised would take it personally and feel upset and annoyed at the other citizen. Within every city or town there are different districts and some people won't like a certain district. Once again the person from the district that was criticised would react in the same way. It is important to understand that while there are differences between all types of people, that there is also a similarity between them.

There is a difference between men and women, between people living in cities and in rural areas, between people of different religions, political traditions, professions and trades. There are large differences between people from different countries. Everyone has a culture in his or her religion, class, occupation, nationality, and sex. However, even though there are differences between all human beings, they still have a lot in common. All of them are members of the human race and while they will differ in many ways, it is always worth remembering that they are similar in many more ways.

It is important to see people as *human beings firstly* and then as the type of person that they are, based on their race, religion, class, occupation, or political affiliation.

Many people are willing to criticise their governments and will say dreadful things about some of their political leaders but when it comes to their country or its institutions, the army, police forces, legal systems, and so on, people get very defensive. Lots of people don't want to accept that *their* country, or a country to which they are strongly committed, has ever done anything wrong. Thankfully we now live in a world where the majority of countries have a harmonious relationship with each other. However, as we all know in the past people representing some countries committed dreadful atrocities. Yet within those countries, there are many people who will deny that their ancestors ever did anything wrong. Regardless of the evidence or proof, they will refuse to believe the facts.

It is not just attacks on people's countries that provoke a negative reaction but criticism of their views. Many years ago I knew a man who was a very strong socialist. He used to get very frustrated when someone criticised socialism, trade unions or other left wing ideals. He denied that there was anything wrong with the beliefs that he held. One of the people who used to criticise him was a very strong supporter of capitalism. He used to get furious when it was criticised. He maintained that there was never any discrimination against working people in the past and that there was never a need for trade unions. Both of these people were so committed to their beliefs that they took any criticism of them very personally.

At that same time I knew a girl who was very committed to the social class system. She considered herself upper class and when anyone criticised the class system, she would get very defensive. She took the criticism of her belief as a criticism of herself.

The same applies to religions, political views and anything that people are strongly committed to. When something that a person feels very committed to is challenged, attacked or rejected, it is not unusual for that individual to take the criticism personally and strongly reject it.

A self-confident person is able to accept criticism of themselves, their country, county, district and all things that they are committed to. They will not take criticism personally.

(d) Blaming People

While all human beings make mistakes from time to time and some can do things that are very wrong, they may resent being blamed for what they have done, and can get very defensive. All the facts, logic or evidence that one can provide will be to no avail and the more the individual is blamed, the more they will defend their actions and reject criticism. There are, of course, exceptions to every rule and there are some people who will accept the blame and admit their errors. Most people, however, will react negatively.

It was outlined earlier that in time the person may mellow and accept that they made mistakes or did things wrong and accept the blame. But while they were being blamed they would have reacted negatively towards the individual who was blaming them. Blaming people is one way of starting an argument, and provoking a defensive reaction.

In the chapter on Conflict Resolution I will outline how it is possible to get someone to accept their mistakes and admit that they may have been wrong.

2. Image

When one thinks of people's image what comes to mind is an individual who is obsessed with their appearance and who wishes to impress others with their clothes, hair style, etc. While these people do exist, not everyone falls into that category. There are lots of people who have little interest in how they look and who prefer to spend their money on food, drink and entertainment, rather than on their appearance. However, many people do have a degree of vanity within them, even if they would not call it that. It is not uncommon to find an individual who would like to be a little taller or smaller, thinner or fatter, to have a smaller nose or ears, more hair etc. They would not be obsessed with their appearance and may even be prepared to joke about it. It is when *other people* comment on their appearance that they get agitated.

Some men who are losing their hair or going grey, may be willing to refer to it themselves. However, if someone else makes a reference to it they can get a little upset. Someone who is overweight may be willing to joke about it but they will not appreciate remarks from others.

An important point to always bear in mind is that we should never assume that other people will react to situations as we would. For example, while I don't mind someone making fun of me, telling a joke at my expense, commenting on my shortcomings, such as the fact that I am small, it would be wrong of me to assume that they would not mind me doing exactly the same thing to them.

People can be sensitive about certain things and unless someone knows the individual very well, they should be careful about what they say to them. Self-confidence is central to this. A very self-confident person who has total faith in themselves and is not dependent on the approval of others, can accept comments and criticism more easily than people who are not very self-confident and are rather sensitive.

3. Fear

Fear is part of the human condition. Most people have fears of different kinds. My main fear is "heights." Going up on a very tall bridge or standing on the roof of a large building can make me feel uncomfortable. Other people have a fear of flying, open or enclosed spaces, dogs, cats, mice or rats, spiders etc. Some of these fears are not a major problem and can be coped with well enough. They can be described as *phobias.*

Fear of speaking in public affects many people. Fear becomes a problem when it influences people's thinking, behaviour or relationships. Fear of failure, fear of rejection, fear of letting oneself down in front of others, fear of making a fool of oneself, these are fears that influence many people. Fear of other people, their personalities, positions, skills or abilities can also affect some individuals.

Fear of failure

It is not uncommon to find a person who is afraid to do something in case they will fail. The shock of accepting defeat is too much for them to take, so the safest way to avoid this is not to try to succeed.

Over the years that I have been training people I have come across individuals who admitted to me that they did not apply for a job because they believed that they would not be appointed to it. Others declined promotions because they were afraid that they would not be able to do the job well. Some people were reluctant to accept positions on committees as they felt that their ideas would not be as impressive as those of the other members.

Fear of Rejection

People don't like to be rejected by others. However, all people are rejected from time to time. There is no easy way to reject another person and the more sensitive the individual is, the harder they will take it. A girl refuses a man's invitation to dance or for a date, an individual ends a relationship, someone is turned down for a job or promotion, is removed from a committee or board or is defeated in an election. All of these are a form of rejection. Everyone likes to win and enjoy victory. However, success can only come when people take risks and taking risks leave people open to being rejected. Another area where rejection can affect people is if there is opposition to things that were recommended by them.

As I said earlier, if an individual is very committed to something, they can be negative towards someone who does not agree to what they are committed to. If one person likes a book or a film or a television programme, and another dislikes it and says why they dislike it, it can make the person who is a supporter of it angry. If someone was to recommend to another person to go to a restaurant which they really liked and they got a negative reaction from the person who visited it, they might feel depressed. There are people who see themselves as ideal human beings. They would like other people to share their views on lots of issues, to agree with things that they are committed to. They can react very negatively towards people who reject their views, commitments, values, or interests. The more self-confident a person is and the more faith that they have in themselves and their abilities, then the easier it is to accept rejection.

Fear of letting oneself down in front of others

Many people like to impress others, and to receive the approval of other individuals for their views, beliefs and things that they have done, or bought or achieved. To be respected by other people is very pleasant and there is nothing wrong in my opinion, with enjoying praise, appreciation or recognition.

However, it is important that one should not be dependent on other people's approval. All people make mistakes from time to time, make bad decisions or fail to achieve something. For the person who is not very confident, it can be a major issue to have to admit defeat or failure to others. They feel that their status has fallen, they will be looked down upon by others, and their self-esteem is lowered.

There can be occasions when it would add to one's problems to openly discuss an error that one made or a failure that one suffered and nobody wants to promote themselves in a negative way, but one should not be influenced by trying to impress other people.

4. Jealousy

While jealousy is a part of human behaviour, it is not something that affects everyone.

Back in the 1970s a young man told me a story that highlighted the issue of jealousy. He played the guitar and brought it along to a party where he intended to entertain the guests. He considered himself a good singer and player. After spending some time talking to people, he suddenly heard a guitar being played and saw a man standing at the top of the room playing and then singing. The audience were very impressed and kept on calling for encores. For the young man in question, it was a very upsetting event. Nobody had asked him to play and he resented the recognition that the player was getting. He told me that he considered the player a show-off and felt that he was a far better guitarist and singer. He left the party early in a very depressed mood. When he did my course in 1973, he admitted to me that he was really jealous of the other young man and wanted to be up there impressing the guests.

Jealousy is a feature of the human condition and some people suffer from it even though they will not admit it. One of the reasons why people criticise others or put them down is that they feel that the other person is better at something than they are. A really confident person can accept the reality of someone being more experienced or professional than they are. It is the individual who is not very assured who will try to put down someone else.

Another area where jealousy can manifest itself is resentment. It is not uncommon to find an individual resenting another because of their ability, talent or achievements.

Years ago a young man who took part on my course told me that he resented some of his friends. He was part of a group of four who socialised together and played golf. Three of these young men were very successful in their careers but the lad who was doing the course had never developed his career. His friends seemed to be always getting new jobs or promotions, and he told me that when this happened he would be very pleased for them but at the same time he also felt resentment, as it never happened to him. He did not like this about himself and that is why he decided to do my course. His main difficulty was a lack of confidence and a fear of attending interviews. The course built up his confidence and he set up his own business and has become a successful person. I met him two years ago and he discussed his attitude to his friends. He now felt a great deal more positive towards them and accepted that his former approach was due to his own low self-esteem.

5. Insecurity

As people go through life they can experience a degree of insecurity from time to time. Insecurity in their jobs, their relationships or in society itself. Once again, confidence is the key to overcoming insecurity.

Some years ago I conducted an in-house course in Communication Skills for a large company and I kept hearing horror stories about a middle ranking manager. He was regarded as rude, ignorant and aggressive. On the final day of the course we all went for a drink in the hotel bar and after a while this man entered the lounge. I was introduced to him and we both sat at the bar discussing the industry etc. After a few drinks he said to me:

"I suppose you got the impression that I wouldn't win a popularity contest with that lot over there."

"Well, I gather that you're not exactly the flavour of the month," I replied, and changed the topic to something more general. After another few sips of his drink he said:

"This is a very difficult company to work for."

"That must be tough for you," I responded and started to change the conversation.

He then had a few more drinks and started telling me about his problems. He was forty-two years of age and had been in the same position for many years. Twice in the preceding two years he had been by-passed for a position that he felt he should have been given. He was very resentful about this, firstly, at the management for not promoting him and then at the two people who had been appointed to these posts. He used to go home every evening to his wife, who had great ambitions for him that she felt he was not living up to. Many of her friends' husbands were very successful men, some were senior managers, directors or had their own companies. She was constantly pushing him to get a better job as she wanted to move to a particular area similar to the districts that her friends lived in. Back at work his managers put him under quite a lot of pressure and the unfortunate man could not cope with the difficulties that he had to live with. He drank a lot while off the job and tended to be aggressive and problematical on the job.

What I began to realise was that the group sitting in the alcove that had just finished my course probably saw the man sitting at the bar with me as a rude, arrogant and aggressive person. What I began to see beside me was a man who was bitter, resentful and very upset that his career had not developed as he had hoped it would. I asked him:

"Do those people over there know what you have just told me?"

"No, they don't," he replied.

"I see," I said. "Let me make a suggestion to you. If you would like to improve your relationship with your staff, it is up to you to take the initiative. Because of the way things are at present, they will be reluctant to approach you as you are their manager, so if you join them at coffee or lunch breaks, and show an interest in them this will contribute to them seeing you in a more positive way."

I met him in my office over a period of time and gave him some ideas on how he could rebuild his relationship with his staff. He was committed to developing his career and things improved for him in the company that he worked in.

In many companies there are people like that. Individuals whose careers have not developed or who suffer from personal problems. They are unhappy people and this affects their relationships with those that they deal with. It is very difficult for people in a company to have to work with someone who is going through a difficult time in their life.

Example:

If I was the manager of a company or a section within an organisation, and a member of my staff was coming in to work over a period in bad form or not working well with their colleagues, then it would be my responsibility to deal with this matter. I could bring the individual into my office, raise the matter with them and maybe help them to find a solution to their problem. If specialist assistance was needed, I could recommend them to some form of counselling. However, if I was an employee in a company and my manager was aggressive and abusive and treated me badly, I could not act in the same way. It would not be possible to meet and raise the matter with the manager, explaining that they had acted badly and they should possibly consider counselling.

I have come across many people on my courses over the years who have had to cope with a manager or supervisor who was difficult. There are no easy or glib solutions for how to handle this situation. This is where what I call "Professionalism" comes into being. By that I mean having the ability to go into work every day no matter how one feels and never to allow problems to affect relationships with others.

We all go to concerts, recitals, plays or shows. Do we ever think of how the performers feel some evenings just before they go on stage? I am sure that there are nights when the last thing that they feel like doing is walking on to the stage and performing for the audience. Like all of us, they can have their problems, such as health problems, relationship problems, financial difficulties or career difficulties. To the audience, they seem to be really enjoying themselves, singing, telling jokes, playing instruments etc. However they could be feeling unwell and are anxious to end their performance. They do not walk on to the stage and say to the audience, "I am not in the best of form tonight so I'm not going to be as good as I normally am." We have paid for a good performance and they will rise to the occasion because they are "professionals."

I have had to develop that skill. There have been many times when I have had problems. In my early days I had a lot of financial difficulties due to the lack of interest in training. That made me feel very upset. Also girls that I was going out with left me and I felt very upset. However, I had to go into my course many nights and conduct it in the right way to the participants. I never allowed my personal problems to affect my training – when I entered the training room I left all of my problems behind me. I recommend this to people who attend my course. While it is not easy and it can be stressful, it contributes to good working relationships. There is also a level of satisfaction to be gained by doing this. At the end of a difficult day or week one can relax and unwind in the knowledge that despite all the difficulties, one has acted professionally.

Dealing with people who are experiencing problems whether at work, in organisations or on a personal level can be very difficult. An individual who has self-confidence and complete faith in themselves can cope with these situations better than someone who is insecure. In the chapter on self-confidence I outlined how to overcome insecurity.

6. Ambition

Most people are ambitious to a certain degree. They want to achieve success in order to improve the quality of their lives. However, it is important that one's ambitions are realistic. The difficulty with some people is that they **think** that they can achieve something even though they do not have the talent or ability. When I use the word ambition I do not see it only as wanting to become a chief executive, a political leader, or a highly successful and wealthy individual. The important thing for people is to find their niche in life. To find a career that they enjoy and that gives them satisfaction. Some people are lucky in this regard but others are not.

The three major things that people need in their lives are the following:

• good health
• the right career
• the right partner.

To be fulfilled & have a purpose in life

For some people, the important thing is their job. These are individuals who have found a career that suits them. It is challenging, stimulating and rewarding and they are very happy doing their work. These are lucky people.

There are others who may not be very interested in their jobs and who may get their satisfaction outside of work. It could be that they belong to an organisation that gives them fulfilment. They may be working for a cause to which they are strongly committed, making a contribution to the less fortunate members of society through a charitable organisation, or working to develop their community through a residents' association. This is their 'raison d'être' and it makes them happy and fulfilled.

For others it is their social life. They may be heavily involved in sport, music, the arts or may just gain fulfilment from socialising with their friends.

There are those whose main purpose in life is their family, husband, wife and children. This gives them happiness and fulfilment.

Then there are those who may have all of these. A career that they enjoy, participation in an organisation that gives them great satisfaction, a good social life and good relationships at home and with their friends. These are the lucky people and the ones that are easiest to deal with. Like all human beings they will have their difficulties and off days, but overall they are easy enough to cope with.

However, there are people who are the exact opposite. Those who have not found a career that suits them or who have failed to make the progress to the level that they aspired. Outside of work they may not have any great interest in anything and perhaps they do not have good relationships with other people.

These people can be more difficult to deal with, and if that is the case, there are no easy ways of handling them. They are unlikely to admit their problems to others and are not aware of the effect that their behaviour has on other people.

Back in 1968, I worked in an organisation for a few months and there was a woman who was my superior and was very difficult to work with. She was aggressive, argumentative and very critical of the staff. She would see people talking at the end of the corridor and would march up, take them down to the office and criticise their performance as employees. Our reaction to her was typical of young people at the time. We called her names, made faces at her behind her back, said what her real problem was and what she really needed. I only spent a short time working with her and I did not meet her again until 1981 when I was having lunch in Bewley's on Grafton Street and she recognised me.

She joined me at my table and we spoke for a while. After a few minutes she said to me:

"You must have found it very difficult working with me, Frank?"

"Why do you say that?" I said.

"Oh, I know that I was hard to work with," she replied and she proceeded to tell me her life story.

She had never married, had spent most of her time looking after her mother who was an invalid. When her mother died, she was in her late thirties and in those days (in the 1960s) women did not have the career opportunities or salaries that thankfully they have now. She spent her working day in a position that she did not enjoy and after work went home to an empty house. She told me how she heard us young people discussing on a Monday morning the exciting weekends that we had at discos and parties, and on Fridays looking forward to going to the local for a few drinks and planning our weekends. She had nothing much to do as most of her friends lived far away or had families to look after. She was very unhappy. In the mid-1970s she did a course in literacy skills and joined a group that went into the poorer sections of Dublin and trained young people to read and write. This gave her a sense of fulfilment and she became a happier person. When I met her, while she was twelve years older, she looked younger.

When she left the restaurant, I remembered thinking about how dreadful her life must have been and if I had known what she had told me when I worked with her, I would have been more charitable in my attitude towards her. In many companies and organisations there are people whose lives are difficult and whose behaviour affects other people. If they find a career or a goal in life, they tend to treat people in a more suitable manner.

To be a good communicator one needs more than just a good command of language. An insight into how people think and behave, and knowledge of what motivates people and contributes to successful communication skills is very important.

An important thing to remember about human behaviour is that most people never blame themselves for things that they do. While, thankfully, the majority of human beings are totally opposed to crime and violence, the people who engage in these activities by and large do not regard themselves as having done bad things. We are aware that all those who have engaged in terrorism, killing people, committing dreadful crimes, regard themselves as good people and believe that they should be able to continue to engage in what they are doing. People are sent to prison for crimes that they committed. I believe that they will sit in their cell cursing the judge for having imprisoned them. They do not regard themselves as bad people and feel that they should be allowed to continue to commit crimes.

Many people leave companies, having been made redundant, dismissed or demoted. They will often be furious towards their employer who had to let them go. They will believe that they should be allowed to keep their job until *they* decide to leave. The fact that they did not do their work well will not be acceptable to *them*.

Over the many years that I have been in business, I have had excellent people working with me. However, there were a few who were not successful and who caused problems for my business and I had to remove them. I know that they hated me and told other people, including their next employer, dreadful things about me. They believed that they should have continued to stay in my company until *they* found a new position. This is human nature.

Back in 1967, I was still in the process of finding a career and I was given a position of a trainee junior executive within a company. I was inexperienced and did not work very well. When my probation period came to an end, I was dismissed. While I was disappointed and very upset, I did not blame my employer. I knew that I was inexperienced due to my age and political involvement. I did not expect my employer to keep me in the company due to the fact that I made too many mistakes and was too radical. I still had a lot of respect for my employer and knew that it was **my** fault that I lost my job.

What I have outlined in this chapter is an insight into human behaviour, how people think, act and react, and the things that motivate people's behaviour.

To be a good communicator one needs more than just a good speaking voice. We all have to deal with people in both our working and personal lives. There is no simple way of getting everything that we want or of convincing others to do what we want them to do. However, having a good knowledge of human behaviour will contribute to people having a more successful relationship with other human beings.

6

Conflict Resolution

As people go through life, there will always be conflicts between individuals. Sometimes these conflicts are of a minor nature and can be resolved easily. However, there are times when major issues are at stake and that can lead to crisis situations developing. There is no simple solution to a major conflict and if it is to be resolved all sides that are involved must be committed to seeking a solution. If one party to the conflict is not committed to finding a solution, then this will extend the problem and make agreement very difficult. The first point to remember is that in most cases each party will regard the other as responsible for the problem and themselves as the innocent victim. Most human beings will never blame themselves no matter how much evidence there may be to prove that they created the problem.

Another important point to keep in mind is that if the conflict is to be resolved, it must be to the satisfaction of all parties. If there are winners and losers, then while the conflict may end it will leave bad feelings among the losers and this can lead to an unsatisfactory conclusion. All people like to win, to beat their opponents and to enjoy victory. In sport, elections, debates or business, that is acceptable. However, in personal relationships where one has to continue to work, do business, sit on committees or boards, or even live with someone after the conflict is over, winning should not be an objective. The good communicator always takes the long-term view and looks to the future when the conflict is over and is committed to either rebuilding the relationship or ending it on a positive note. When human beings are involved in difficult situations with others, it is easy to let one's emotions take over and influence one's behaviour.

The first thing to be conscious of is the attitude that one adopts towards the individual with whom there is a problem. It can be very difficult to be friendly or to convey the impression that while there is a difference between both sides on the issue, it is not of a personal nature. If someone is very angry with another person because of what was done, it is only natural for that person to see the conflict as a personal issue. The difficulty with that is that the conflict will go on longer and will take more time to resolve. The more one knows about the personality and temperament of the individual on the opposite side, the better off one is. Dealing with an individual who is a stranger is more complicated as it is difficult to know how they will react. Therefore, before approaching the person to raise the issue one should be conscious of the importance of not bringing things down to a personal level, and should try to adopt as positive an attitude as possible.

Preparation

Many people approach others to raise matters in an unprepared way. They feel very strongly about what has happened and tend to be too emotional. To succeed in resolving a conflict, spending time preparing for the meeting is the answer. The first thing to bear in mind is that there is no easy way to find a solution. There may have to be many meetings with little progress being made at each one. Secondly, it is important to be prepared for the other person to refuse to accept that they have been responsible for what has happened and to expect them to blame someone else. Most people do not like to be blamed for what they have done and rationalise their activities no matter how dreadful. As part of the preparation, try to see the issue from the perspective of the other person and ascertain how they might react when the issue is raised. This can be difficult as it is natural for people to see things from their own perspective only and to try and put oneself into the frame of mind of a person to whom one is strongly opposed is not easy.

A person can read in the papers or hear through the media of a dispute between management and workers in a company. Because it does not affect them, they can be very objective about the dispute. They can see and understand both sides of the argument, even if they believe that one side is right. However, if they were involved in the dispute either as a member of the management side or as an employee, they would probably see things only from their own perspective and totally oppose the other side. That is normal behaviour and most people fall into that category. So as part of the preparation for resolving conflicts, always expect the other side to adopt a hostile attitude. If they don't, one has an advantage and this can lead to a satisfactory solution at an earlier stage. As well as being prepared for the attitude that might be adopted, also make a list of what may be said and prepare the responses that could be used to deal with the issues. The importance of preparation is essential.

In the chapter on presentation skills, I will emphasise the necessity of good preparation and outline how confident and effective the speaker will be if they are in control of the situation. The same principle applies in dealing with conflicts. If the individual is well prepared, they will feel a lot more confident about approaching the other side, raising the issues and dealing with reactions.

Tone of Voice and Body Language

An essential element in approaching people in conflict situations is tone of voice and manner of speaking. Most people do not know how they speak; the voice that they hear when talking can sound different to those who are listening. While many people may have heard their voices on tape recorders, or on videos if doing courses, it may not be the same tone that they use when speaking to people. One factor that can influence the tone of voice is mood. Anger, frustration, tension or outrage can change the way in which the voice will come across to the listener. While the person who is talking may think that they are behaving normally, the listener can feel that they are being verbally attacked or put down. It is not always easy to control the tone of voice when one is upset or defensive. However, if one is conscious of the advantage of speaking in a positive and constructive tone, then the environment between both sides will be more relaxed.

Another thing that can influence what one is saying is how people use their hands. Anger, tension and outrage can result in the individual coming across as aggressive, which will be unsettling for the person who is being approached. When an individual is being spoken to and they see the speaker using their hands in an aggressive way, it can influence how they react to what is being said. Another important point is the use of eye contact and facial expression. If the speaker is staring too hard, with the face twisted or painful looking, it can affect what they are saying. Maintaining good eye contact and avoiding sending negative signals through one's face will contribute to the other person being less opposed to the speaker. So in order to create the right environment when discussing an issue that is difficult, always be conscious of the tone of voice that is used, how the hands are treated and the necessity of establishing proper eye contact and facial expression.

Listening

A very important aspect of communications is the ability to listen when someone is speaking. One reason why some people don't listen is that the speaker fails to hold their attention. In the area of discussing issues that can cause problems between people, listening is essential. However, if someone is saying something that an individual is strongly opposed to, it is possible that the person who is being addressed is not listening to all of what is being said but formulating their own response. If a person is being criticised or the values to which they are committed are being rejected, it is understandable that they will be upset and may start to mentally decide what to say in response.

In trying to resolve a conflict, listening to the other side without displaying a negative reaction, visually or verbally, is essential. While it is not wrong to reject someone's views or opinions, the manner in which it is done is vital. In a conflict situation it is possible that both sides are in an emotional state and this can influence how they respond to each other. It is not easy to listen clearly to what the opposite side is saying as most people take things personally and will be inclined to think that the speaker is criticising them and not just their views or what they may have done. In order to resolve a conflict, it is necessary to build a rapport with the other side. One of the best ways to achieve this is to listen to what is being said and not interrupt the speaker.

Drawing it all together

When a person is well prepared for a meeting with an individual, it will make them more confident and more able to deal with the situation. The first thing to do is to greet the individual by name, in the right tone of voice, and to outline that one hopes to sort things out. For example, "Good evening, Frank. Thank you for meeting me to discuss our problem. I hope we can sort it out to the satisfaction of both of us." If Frank was to react in a different way by sounding negative or aggressive it is essential not to take it personally. If both people are good communicators and are committed to sorting out problems in a constructive way, then it will be easier to make progress. If only one person is tactful and diplomatic, then it can be a more challenging situation.

A mistake that people make is to talk too much and indicate that they are right and their opponent is wrong. When the discussion starts it is useful to let the other person start talking and give their views on the issue. It is essential not to interrupt them or send a signal that one believes that they are incorrect. Due to the fact that both sides will not agree with each other, it is not right to tell the other person that they are wrong in what they said or did. It would be better to ask them why they did what they did. Asking people to outline what they did and why they did it, in the right tone of voice, is more tactful than telling them what they did and why they should not have done it.

It is very negative to blame someone for having done something. People do not like to be blamed and they can take it very personally. Telling people to do something can also get a negative reaction. It is more effective to ask them to consider doing something. While most people do not like being told what to do, they are willing to consider making a change if it is put to them in the right way.

It is essential to avoid arguments. It is better for people to talk **to** rather than **at** each other. To resolve a conflict with a person who is rational and reasonable is a lot easier than with someone who is irrational or unstable. Some people are willing to accept that they have shortcomings and may be willing to concede that they have made a mistake or done something wrong. However, there are also individuals who are the exact opposite and who see themselves as never being wrong in what they have done.

It is not easy to deal with the latter group and even if one was to use all the skills that I outlined, it would probably not work. If a person who is sober is trying to sort out a problem with someone who is drunk, it would be very difficult due to the mentality of the person who was drunk. It is the same when dealing with a person who is very insecure, unstable, with little faith in themselves. The only way to try to make progress when dealing with a very difficult person is to get a third party to act as an independent assessor.

What I have outlined in this chapter is based on what I devised when I had to sort out problems with many people in the challenging years that I had in the 1970s. What I have outlined has worked for me in most situations and I included it in my course in the 1980s. Many people have found that it helped them to resolve conflicts.

The fact that a person is a very good communicator, is very confident and knows how to deal wtih conflict situations does not mean that they will find all potentially difficult situations simple, and always achieve what they want. However, they will be able to cope better.

The chapters on negotiation skills and meetings will outline how to meet with people to whom one is opposed and sort out disagreements. There is a similarity between resolving conflicts and negotiating. This section of the book makes participants more effective when they have to sort out problems and deal with difficult individuals. While it is never easy to have to face these situations, it helps a great deal to possess the ability to do so.

7

Decision-making and Problem-solving

As people go through life they are likely to experience problems in both their personal and work situations. There is no easy way to sort out problems and make effective decisions. The longer problems go on the more difficult they can be to sort out. When people are under pressure their minds tend not to function as quickly or as effectively as usual. In today's world most people live under a considerable degree of pressure for various reasons. There is the student studying for exams and worrying about the future; the person going for an interview, feeling tense and nervous; the businessperson experiencing great difficulty in these competitive and uncertain times. Then there are the emotional problems: love, sickness, and death.

During the course of our lives we experience many of these difficulties and yet we survive – sometimes seemingly against the odds. But even though we get over these problems, the prolonged worry can leave scars. Because worry is so prevalent we have come to accept it as part of life and see no way of avoiding it. In fact, we may be somewhat cynical towards anyone who advocates a way of life free from worry. However, if we examine the whole question of worry in an objective way we may surprise ourselves. For example, if we were to ask ourselves what we were worrying about many months ago, in some instances, we may not be able to remember. But we were worrying. It is essential to distinguish between problems and difficulties.

A problem only becomes such when one fails to cope with it. Until then it is only a difficulty. It is the inability to cope with what life hands out to people that drives some of them to excessive drinking, drug-taking and even suicide. Anyone who says that people can go through life without difficulties, setbacks, obstacles and tragedies is talking nonsense. What I am outlining here is a method of controlling many situations and solving many problems at their very outset. The longer we live and the more responsibility we accept the greater the burden we have to carry. But the more positively we think and the more disciplined our minds become, the more effective we will be as individuals.

The method of solving practical difficulties is totally different from how we would handle difficulties of an emotional nature. Let us first look at a number of situations in the practical area and see if we can remedy them.

Practical Difficulties

A useful point to make about finding a solution to a problem is that one should firstly identify the cause of the problem. For example, if the computer system in an office was to break down and an engineer was brought in to fix it, they would have to identify the cause of the problem before they could repair it. If a car fails to start, a mechanic will have to identify the cause of the difficulty before it can be fixed. If a person becomes ill, the doctor will have to identify the cause of the illness before the method of curing it is implemented. I came up with this approach years ago when I went through a difficult situation. Throughout my life I have experienced a lot of problems yet I overcame them because I learned how to cope with crisis situations. When I was young and things went wrong I reacted like many people and worried about the problems. However, I set up my business and developed a system which helped me to stay in control and enabled me to take action to survive.

My first problem came in the early 1970s. When I set up my communications course in 1972 I did not have a lot of money and there was very little interest in communication skills in those days. All the people who came on my course were private individuals. Companies did not send many people on courses until the late 1980s. While I was experienced as a trainer I did not have experience in marketing and selling. I placed advertisements in the *Evening Press* newspaper and that brought people on my communications course which was the only course that I had at *that* time. The numbers attending each session were very small and the fee that I charged was also small. I allowed people to pay the fee on a weekly basis and that added to my problems. Some people got very frightened about standing up and speaking and they did not continue to attend the course. This led to me losing money. Many of the people who came on my course used buses to get to the venue, and there were a lot of bus strikes in Dublin in the early 1970s, and that also caused me a major problem. When the strikes started a lot of people who had joined the course could not attend due to the distance they would have had to travel to get to my office.

By the end of 1973 I was going through a crisis. I owed a lot of money to the newspaper for the advertisements that I had placed. I also owed money for the rent of the office that I had. 1974 was the worst year that I ever had. The number of people who came on my courses was very small and I had a lot of debts. I became very worried and spent a lot of time in great depression. I wanted to have more people on my course but I did not have the ability to get them. Many nights I lay in bed worrying about my crisis and trying to find a solution. I informed many of my friends about how bad things were and some of them told me to stop doing the course and to get a job elsewhere.

While many jobs were available in the 1970s, I did not want to abandon my career, as I loved the work that I was doing. It was the first time that I had been involved in a career that fascinated me. The big shortcoming that I had was that I was looking for a solution to my problem but I had not identified the cause of my problem. Things became worse in May of that year. I had two courses scheduled for Monday the 20th and Thursday the 23rd. The income that would come in would have helped me to survive for the summer months.

The office that I rented was Number 4, North Great Georges Street. A man made an appointment to meet me there on the evening of Friday, 17 May in order to register for the Monday course. I left the office earlier to go to the Gresham Hotel for a cup of tea and I then left the hotel and walked up Parnell Street towards my office. There was a long bus strike on at that time and the traffic was very heavy. I arrived at the corner of Marlborough Street and stood beside a parked car for over a minute waiting for the traffic to pass. I looked at my watch and saw that I would be late for my meeting so I dashed across the street and turned into North Great Georges Street. I had just turned the corner when the car I had been standing beside blew up.

This was one of the dreadful bombs that went off in Dublin that day in connection with the Northern Ireland situation. Thankfully I was not killed or injured but the effects of the bombing caused me a huge problem. People were afraid to go into the city centre for a long time. No one turned up to my courses on the Monday or Thursday. I had no courses for the rest of the summer.

For the next few months I went through the worst crisis of my life and I worried a great deal. I got a lot of assistance from my family but I found it hard to sleep and I was very depressed. In desperation one night in July I got out of bed at two o'clock in the morning and started to look at the dreadful situation that I was in. I sat down at the kitchen table and took a few pieces of paper and started writing out the reasons why I was having my problems. The first point that I wrote was: "Define the problem." I knew the answer: "Not enough people are coming on my course." The second point that I wrote was: "Why are people not coming on the course?" I then began to define the cause of my problems. There were a number of reasons why not enough people were attending.

The first was that I had no experience in the area of marketing and I placed advertisements in a newspaper. The advertisements were not very effective and many people who saw them would not become interested in applying for the course. The second reason was the area where I conducted the course did not attract too many people. While the houses in North Great Georges Street are among the finest houses in Dublin, the area was not as sophisticated then as it is now. In those days the North side of Dublin was not as popular as the South side. Another difficulty was that cars that were parked in the area were often broken into and that led to bad publicity. A leading newspaper used to write articles on what was called the "Bugsy Malones" in relation to people who smashed windows and stole handbags. This would have put many people off attending my course, as they would be reluctant either to park their car nearby or to walk up from the city centre.

The third reason why not enough people joined my course was that I put them off when they contacted me. I was confident and had no difficulty standing up and speaking. When I got phone calls from people I used to tell them how the course would be conducted so that they would become very confident. I told them that they would have to stand up and make speeches of different kinds, that I would get them to speak on an impromptu basis and that they would have to defend standpoints on various issues, including some in which they did not necessarily believe, under question from the other people on the course.

I therefore knew why not enough people were coming on my course:

1. My advertising was ineffective.

2. The area that I was located in was likely to put people off attending.

3. I was talking too much, and in the wrong way, about how the course would be conducted.

The third point that I wrote was: "How can I change the way things are?" The first potential change I could make was in the area of advertising. I realised that if I had an advertising company to design my advertisements, then this would serve to attract more people to my course. The second point I could change was the area where I had my office. I thought that if I had an office on the South side of the city then more people would be prepared to come on the course. Thirdly, if I stopped giving too much detail on how the course was conducted and instead asked every caller to come to meet me I could impress them with my speaking skills and outline the benefits that they would gain from attending.

I then knew the cause of my problems and the potential solutions to them. I then went through how I could use these methods. On another sheet of paper I wrote down the strengths and weaknesses of the three methods.

The main weakness of the first solution was that I could not afford to take on an advertising company. However, on the plus side I could think about how to suggest to a company that it might be worth their while assisting me. The main weakness of the second solution was that I could not afford to move to an office on the South of the city. The rents were too high and I would not have been able to afford it. I could still, however, at least think about how to move to the South side.

The next morning I went through the Golden Pages and looked under the "Advertising" section. I saw the name "Arks" and I telephoned the company and arranged a meeting. When I told the man that I met about my problems I asked him if he would give me advice and that I would pay him within a few months if his advertisement attracted more people. I also told him that I would send him a letter promising to pay. He agreed and devised a very good advertisement. I then went through the "Language Colleges" in the Golden Pages and approached a language college called "Inlingua" at 12, Clare Street, next door to the Mont Clare Hotel. I asked the manager if I could rent one room for three nights a week. He agreed and I was given a price that was reasonable. I now had a very good advertisement and an address in Clare Street.

When the training season started in September, I put the advertisement into a number of papers with the phone number of my apartment. Both the advertisement and the address attracted many people. I requested that they would come to meet me and I did not frighten them by telling them how challenging the course would be. Instead, I outlined how the skills that they would pick up would benefit them. The first course took place on the third Thursday of September and twenty people came on it. The second one started on the first week in October and twenty-five people came. Within a few weeks all my debts were cleared and I was making a good living.

Over the remaining years I had difficult situations but I always used the method that I devised:

1. Think: do not worry.

2. Write down the main reasons why there is a problem, or why things have not worked out as you had hoped.

3. Go through the strengths and weaknesses of the potential solutions.

4. Make the right decisions.

By using these methods I have been able to solve many problems and that is how I have survived in my business. Many people who have done my course have used this method and it has been of great benefit to them. On the course that I conduct I go through this system in great detail.

Emotional Difficulties

What I am going to deal with in this section is how to cope with emotional problems. What I will outline now is based on what I recommended to a man who was going through a major crisis. He was a very well known businessman and he told me the following story.

He was at a reception in a hotel and he was enjoying the occasion. The waiter was walking around filling the glasses with wine. He was a great lover of red wine and he drank a lot of it. When the event came to an end, he left the hotel and got into his Mercedes and drove home. Driving along the Merrion Road he was stopped by the Gardai and breathalysed. He was very much over the limit. The next morning when he woke up he became aware of the crisis that he was going through. While he did not mind paying a heavy fine, he became very depressed about losing his licence, as he had to use his car a lot in his job. Worse still would be the publicity that the case would attract when it came up in court. Because he was well known, he knew that his case would attract media attention and he would then be seen as a drunken driver by all the people who read about it or heard it on the radio or television. His status and reputation would be undermined by what he had done.

For the next few weeks he went through a dreadful crisis. He found it hard to sleep and was very depressed. He worried a great deal about what was going to happen. A friend of his had done my course and recommended that he contact me for assistance. A week before the court case came up, he was feeling very upset and one night in desperation he came to my office when I ended the evening course and asked me if I could help him to cope. I asked him if he had gone through all the things that could occur with his solicitor. He outlined to me what his solicitor had told him. He would not be sent to prison. He would be heavily fined, would lose his licence and because he was well known he would get bad publicity.

I suggested to him that it would be a good idea to try to prepare himself mentally and psychologically for what would happen. The first thing to do was to ask himself, "What is the worst thing that can occur?" He knew the answer. He would lose his licence and get bad publicity. The second thing to do was to see if he could do anything to reduce the damage. He then said to himself, "What can I do to stop this happening?" He knew that he could not do anything. He then accepted that he was going to be reduced in status and that his reputation would be lowered.

For the next week he prepared himself mentally and psychologically for the worst thing that could occur to him. He told me that once he had accepted that he was going to suffer badly and that he could do nothing to alter the situation, he began to feel less upset about it. Over the next week he was still concerned but not devastated about what was going to happen. He had come to accept it.

On a Wednesday morning the court case came up and he arrived at the court feeling upset, as anyone would be in a similar situation. His main concern was the bad publicity that he would get. He looked around the courtroom to see if any journalists were there. The previous night a major political crisis had developed and the media were using up all their resources coping with it. He got no publicity at all. While he was heavily fined and he lost his licence, he did not do as badly as he had expected. Asking these questions helped him reduce the pressure he had:

Question One: What is the worst thing that can occur?

Question Two: Is there anything I can do to stop it happening?

I used the second question myself on two occasions and it helped me. If one can not stop something happening, the only way to cope with it is to try to mentally prepare oneself for what is likely to happen.

It is not easy to do this, as there is no simple way of coping with a crisis situation. However, if one can do it, it is better than spending a lot of time worrying, lacking in sleep and relaxation, and perhaps adversely affecting one's relationships with other people. When I found that this worked for me on two occasions and also for that man, I included it in my communications course.

In 1992 I was brought into a large company which was going through a major crisis in order to assist the staff. A lot of people who came on my course were threatened with possible redundancy. When the course came to an end the participants spoke about how they had benefited from it. A group told me that while they found all the content interesting, the area that impressed them most was the section on problem solving. It helped them to cope with the crisis that they were having. One manager told me the following story.

For over a year he was very worried about losing his job and it had a very negative effect on both his working and personal life. He used to go out with some of his colleagues at the weekend and they all talked about how bad things were. His main concern was that he may have problems getting another job due to his age, and he was consequently worried about whether he would be able to pay the mortgage and meet his other financial commitments. When I covered the section on problem solving he started thinking about how to apply it to his own situation. He asked himself the first question: "What is the worst thing that can occur?" He knew the answer. He could be made redundant. He then asked himself the second question: "Is there anything I can do to stop it happening?" Again he knew the answer. The decision would not be his and it would be taken by a senior executive.

When he accepted that he would be made redundant he started to mentally and psychologically prepare himself for what would happen. He said to me: "For the past year I have been worrying a lot about losing my job. However, over the past month I have been planning to deal with the problem. While I still want to keep my job I am preparing to find a new career." One of the things that he was exploring was setting up his own small company. Two of his colleagues who were also in the same position were assisting him in this area. When I met him after two months he was still employed but he looked and felt a lot more at ease because he had stopped worrying and agonising and was spending time planning for his future. The company that he worked in sorted out its problems and he was kept in his job to his satisfaction. What he found was that the final three months of the crisis were easier to cope with than the previous twelve months, due to him using the method I outlined to him.

As I have stated, it is never easy to cope with a crisis situation and it is natural for people to be very upset and depressed. While there is no guarantee that any system will help to eliminate a major problem, it is useful to try to use the method that I have recommended. If it contributes to reducing the level of stress – a major problem in today's fast-moving world – then it is worth trying.

One of the greatest fears that people have is "Fear of the Unknown" — not knowing what is going to happen. In 1974 a man who attended one of my courses told me a story.

In the 1950s he became ill and went to his doctor. The doctor told him that he wanted him to go to a specialist. He made an appointment and he got the result of the examination a number of days later. He had tuberculosis, which was then a major illness in Ireland. He told me that from the time his doctor told him to go to a specialist until he got the result that he was very depressed. When he heard that he had TB, he was very concerned but he did not feel as bad because he knew what his problem was. It was the period of not knowing what the situation was that was the most difficult for him. That is very understandable.

If a person working in a company is told by a manager early in the morning that they were to meet to discuss a problem at the end of the working day, the employee would find that very upsetting and it would be a very unpleasant working day for them. When the problem is raised, the employee could feel less upset due to the fact that at least they know what has happened and can start to cope with it. It is not knowing what might happen that makes people feel most uncomfortable.

In the late 1920s the United States of America went through a dreadful economic crisis and this had a very bad effect on the American people. One of the most outstanding American presidents, Franklin D. Roosevelt, said, "We have nothing to fear but fear itself." It is my belief that there is no easy way to deal with crisis situations. However, I have used the methods described above, and when they worked for me I recommended them to people who have done my courses and I have got a very good reaction.

8

Meetings

The success of a meeting is influenced by the choice of chairperson. If the chairperson is effective then the meeting will be effective. It does happen that people take over the position of chairperson because they are managers of a department or that they have been members of the committee for a considerable period of time. If the committee is a very civilised one with no rows, arguments or people abusing each other, then most people can be an effective chairperson even if they don't possess the skills necessary for successfully chairing meetings.

There is a difference between business meetings and meetings of social groups, clubs or organisations. This chapter will concentrate on the skills that a chairperson should have, and also outline how people who attend meetings should present their ideas, and persuade and convince others to accept their ideas. It will also cover how to reject other people's ideas in a firm and effective way.

All of the skills that are outlined in this chapter come from my own experience of both chairing and attending meetings since I was very young. I chaired many meetings in a lot of the organisations that I was involved in.

The Role of The Chairperson

In order to be effective, the chairperson must be seen by all in attendance to be fair and impartial. If the chairperson is perceived as taking sides on an issue then this will undermine their credibility and lose the respect of those who oppose the side that the chairperson favours.

While a chairperson is likely to have an opinion on every issue, it is better to keep their views to themselves until the participants reach agreement. Another important duty for the chairperson is to maintain an equal rapport with all the members of the committee. If the chairperson is seen as too closely associated with an individual or a group, especially if those are very influential and persuasive, then this can cause a problem.

I learned this lesson back in 1969. I was chairman of a committee in my local parish and had eight people on the panel. We were producing a magazine in connection with the Parochial Democratic Movement that I set up to oppose my clergy on the parish hall committee system, which was outlined in the chapter on how I developed my skills. Three of the people on the committee were personal friends of mine and they were very good speakers and had a lot of influence. Because they were so good, I let them control the meeting and do all the talking. The other people on the committee were not as good at speaking and had less to say. I used to let them say very little. When the meeting ended, I would join my three friends and we would go to a local pub for a drink. In the pub we discussed the kind of things that young people do. However, I discovered that the other members of the committee saw me as part of a clique and they believed that I was planning the next meeting with my friends. I was very surprised to hear that, but because the individuals were convinced that I was misbehaving, it undermined my reputation and my success as a chairperson was badly affected.

Many years later I was chairing a different committee and once again I was very friendly with two people who were very good speakers and had a lot of influence. When I entered the room I would greet all members of the committee and I did not permit my friends to dominate the meeting. I ensured that all the participants were treated equally and when the meeting ended I would not spend time talking to my friends. Instead, I would approach the people who were less effective at the meetings and I built a good rapport with them. This contributed to my success as a chairperson.

This point is worth considering if ever a chairperson is very friendly with an individual who is very persuasive and who talks a great deal. It is possible that other members of the committee may see the chairperson as being biased or impartial.

There are often two types of people who attend meetings. The ones who do all the talking and who have a lot of influence and those who do not speak much and don't have much influence.

There are a number of reasons why some people do not talk much at meetings:

- They may not be very knowledgeable on the issues that are being discussed.
- They may not be very good at presenting themselves.
- They may be less confident than the other members.
- They may be less senior in the company or organisation than the

other members.

- They may be a lot younger than the other members.

The effective chairperson will always control the dominant members and encourage the quieter ones. When people are asked to make a contribution, they will be willing to do so. However, some people are reluctant to assert themselves and defer to the more confident people.

When I was 13 years of age I was a member of the Legion of Mary and I used to attend the weekly meeting that was held in my school. Due to my lack of confidence at the time and the fact that I was very young I would sit quietly at the table and was afraid to talk or raise issues. When the chairman requested me to give a report on the social work that I had done, I did so. However, I spent the rest of the meeting sitting and listening. Even though I had thoughts on the issues that were being discussed, I was reluctant to present them.

It is very disappointing for a person to leave a meeting feeling that they have achieved very little. The effective chairperson will be very committed to ensuring that all the people in attendance are satisfied that they are making a positive contribution to the committee or organisation.

Some years ago a girl was doing my course and she told me a story about a situation at work that was causing her a problem. Her employer had organised a monthly meeting of staff to deal with various work situations. He appointed this girl to the role of chairperson and he attended the meeting for some time. He wanted the employees to discuss the issues that he raised. When he was in attendance most of the staff said very little and no one disagreed with his opinions. He used to leave the meeting early to return to his office and when he left the discussion really started. They talked a lot and sometimes wanted to change decisions that were made. The chairperson found this difficult as she felt that she was not chairing the meeting properly. She said to me "I can't tell my boss not to talk so much or to ask him to hold off so I can get the members of the staff involved. What advice could you give me to become a better chairperson?" I gave her advice and she contacted her employer and arranged a meeting with him. She did what I told her to do. She said:

"I am sure you are aware that there is not a lot of discussion at our monthly staff meetings."

"Yes", he said, "they don't have much to say." She then said:

"Are you aware that most of your employees are reluctant to oppose your ideas or to publicly disagree with you?" He said, "Oh, are they?" She replied:

"I believe they are. Could I ask you when you were at their level, would you have opposed your employer or disagreed with him in front of your colleagues?"

"Well, we did not have these kind of meetings when I was younger. Would you prefer if I did not attend the meetings?" he asked.

"I am very pleased that you do attend because you make a very good contribution," she said. "Could I make a suggestion to you? If I was to send you a signal would you agree to holding back so that I could get the members to contribute to the issues that are being discussed?"

"Oh, yes", he replied, "I would like them to be more constructive and involved."

For the next few meetings, things worked out very well. The chairperson would send a signal, such as a movement of her hand or an eye movement and the employer would stop talking and she would go around the group asking each person to give their opinions. After a while, a major issue arose and because of his position as Chief Executive, the employer had to revert back to his method of dominating the meeting. The chairperson became concerned and she made an appointment to meet with him. She said, "I am fully aware that you had to deal with the matters that we discussed at our last two meetings, due to your position. You did a very good job in sorting things out. I would like to ask you to consider re-establishing the arrangement that we came to some weeks ago, whereby I will send you a signal so that I can get the group involved." Being a reasonable person, he agreed and things improved a lot.

One can not criticise one's employer or manager or tell them what to do. However, asking people to *consider* doing something and making *suggestions* to them, in a positive way, is acceptable.

When I outlined this story on a number of my courses several participants who were senior managers informed me that they had behaved similarly at staff meetings and that what I covered made them change their behaviour. It is very easy for a person who is in a senior position in a company or organisation or who is very confident and a good presenter to dominate the meeting. It is also difficult for the chairperson to perform properly if one of the participants is more senior than they are – but the chairperson is the individual who has to control the meeting and conduct it effectively. If an individual who attends the meetings is more senior to the chairperson in the company or organisation, they should defer to them and not upstage them in front of the committee.

Another difficulty that can arise at a meeting is that it can go on too long. Too much time is spent on the issues on the agenda and some of the committee members can lose interest. The reason why this happens is that the meeting has not been planned correctly. The effective chairperson will prepare for the meeting and will be committed to ensuring that all the participants will find it interesting. While there is no exact time for all meetings to take place, it is essential to structure it to suit the group that is attending. The following is a useful way to organise and control a meeting.

If the chairperson would like to confine the meeting to one hour, this is how it can be arranged.

Each member of the committee will be requested to send in a list of the issues that they would like to have discussed, to the committee secretary. They will also be given a date and a time to do so. For example, if a meeting is to take place on a Friday from 4.00 p.m. to 5.00 p.m., then the committee members will be asked to forward the list by perhaps 5.00 p.m. on a day prior to the meeting. When the lists are sent to the secretary, they will be forwarded to the chairperson who will then draw up the agenda. If there were six items to be discussed, the chairperson will allot a time limit to deal with each item.

Item number one might in the opinion of the chairperson be worth a ten-minute discussion period. They will write in 10 beside that point. The second item may be assumed to be worth a fifteen-minute discussion, 15 will be written beside that point. The third item might be worth another ten minutes and another 10 will be placed beside that point. The remaining items will be given a similar figure for discussion based on the view of the chairperson.

The agenda with the figures placed on it should only be kept by the chairperson. The agenda that is sent to the committee members or placed on the table at the meeting does not require the time limit for each item to be written. The meeting now commences.

The first issue that can be raised is a report from the secretary on the last meeting. The secretary should prepare the report and ensure that all the important issues that were raised are referred to and the decisions that were taken are outlined. The chairperson then seeks a reaction from the members on the report. If a member disagrees with what they were reported to have said or done, they are entitled to raise that issue. The manner in which they do it is essential. The good communicator will not get aggressive and start a row. They will outline in a constructive way what they said or did. A discussion can develop on that issue.

Another thing that the secretary should do is to make a list of the people who are attending the meeting and those who have apologised for missing it. The chairperson then starts the meeting. It is essential to ensure that the discussions are focused on the items that are raised. The more people that there are attending the meeting can lead to some raising matters that are further down the agenda or not on the agenda at all.

When an item is being discussed it is possible that people will disagree with each other on it. That is perfectly acceptable. There is nothing wrong with people opposing one another on an issue. In my opinion, disagreement is a positive thing. If everyone is to agree on every issue no progress will be made. It is **how** one disagrees that is vital. In the section on "Presentations at Meetings", I will outline how to oppose someone's ideas and reject them in a positive, constructive manner.

The chairperson has now raised the first item to which 10 minutes has been given. As was outlined earlier, the chairperson will ensure that everyone can make a contribution. If a disagreement is raised, the chairperson will maintain control and not permit people to get personal with each other. If a committee is experiencing problems and there are a lot of arguments and rows occurring, then the chairperson should reorganise the system at the first meeting that they chair. If an individual takes over the role of chairperson from their predecessor and continues to conduct the meeting in the same way, then things may not change. If after several meetings the new chairperson decides that they want to stop the rows and bring about changes, then it could be difficult to achieve that. The ideal situation is for the new chairperson to outline how the meetings will be conducted at the **FIRST** meeting that they will chair. The way to do this is as follows:

"I am now going to outline how these meetings will be conducted during my term as chairperson. As you all know, over the past few months, there have been a lot of unpleasant meetings due to disagreements that have taken place between us. While I am committed to a full and frank discussion of the issues, I am not going to allow anyone to get personally abusive. We are here to discuss issues to the benefit of our organisation. If anyone starts to get abusive, I will order him or her to withdraw their personal comments and apologise to the individual that has been abused. If the individual refuses to accept my recommendation, I will call a halt to the meeting."

Adopting this approach can contribute to people altering the manner in which they behave as most would not want to be seen as responsible for the meeting being cancelled. I had to do this several times years ago, when I chaired meetings that were very controversial. The method that I devised worked very well.

As stated earlier the first item on the agenda was given 10 minutes. As the time is coming to an end the chairperson will monitor how things are going. If the matter has been discussed to the satisfaction of the committee and no one has anything else that they wish to mention, then the chairperson will end the discussion and if a decision has to be taken, call a vote. If the decision has to be implemented, an individual or a group will be appointed to do so.

If, however, a larger range of issues on the item were raised, then it would be wrong to end the discussion. When the chairperson was setting up the agenda they put a time that they **thought** would be appropriate to devote to the item. It is possible that a longer time should have been given. By ending the discussion some of the committee may become concerned that they did not have an opportunity to raise matters that they had wanted to. That could cause a difficulty.

To deal with this matter the chairperson has three options.

1. They can let the meeting go on for an extra period of time and cover the entire agenda.

2. If they want to keep the meeting to the **one** hour, they could decide to give the time allotted to another item which they believe could be deferred until the next meeting. For example, item number three does not need to be raised today so its 10 minutes can now be transferred to the current item.

3. If the item is very important a special meeting can be arranged to deal with it.

When the meeting comes to an end the chairperson should mention:

All the issues that were discussed and outline the decisions that were made and what has been agreed. It is possible at some meetings to have the issue of "A.O.B., (Any other business)" on the agenda. This can raise too many issues and can lead to the meeting going on too long.

The final item would be to give the date, time and venue of the next meeting and the date by which items that people want to raise should be sent to the secretary.

I have always said that there is just one disadvantage of being a really good chairperson and that is that one will be reappointed to the position again and again.

Making presentations at meetings

This section will now concentrate on the people who attend the meetings. Presentation is not just standing up with an overhead projector. When people sit around a table at a meeting they are making presentations.

There are similarities in both methods of presentation. They are as follows:

1. Preparing for the meeting. This aspect deals with the preparation that should be made before one attends the meeting.
2. Presentation at the meeting. This deals with the manner in which one presents ideas, and how one can hold the interest of other people and convey their ideas, without ambiguity, misinterpretation or unnecessary repetition.

The third area, which relates specifically to attending and presenting at meetings, is that one is endeavouring to influence and persuade other members to accept one's ideas, and reject or modify other people's ideas.

When people go to a meeting they may **feel** strongly about an issue. However, it is essential that they should be aware of the objections that will be raised to what they are committed to and how they will cope with them.

Because people are very committed to what they will speak about, it is essential to accept that other individuals will have a different view and to know what objections will be raised and how to deal with the objections. This is where the **preparation for the meeting** is important.

The following is an outline of a meeting that could take place and how to deal with it. It is based on the session that I cover on my Training Programme.

If I was the production manager in a company and one of my staff left but was not replaced, I and the other staff members would be under a lot of pressure due to the resulting shortage of staff. We would all be working longer hours. I would want to get an extra person in my department. I have had a number of meetings with my employers request-ing that I be given an extra person. When I had my meetings with the senior managers, I made a major issue of the long hours that I and my staff have had to work, the pressure that we are all experiencing and I am asking that I be given what **I** want. However, while my employers are anxious to assist me, they have their own agenda and for reasons that they are committed to, they are not able to give me what **I** want.

The reason why I have failed to get an extra member for my depart-ment is due to the fact that I have been talking about what **I** want and why they should accept **my** recommendations and do what **I** want them to do. This is a mistake that many people make when they are trying to convince other people to accept their recommendations. It is under-standable that people **feel** strongly about things, believe that **they** are right and expect other people to agree with them. However, everyone has a different outlook and sees things from their own perspective. While many people would like to assist others, they will be motivated by what is best for **themselves**.

Having failed to persuade my employers to give me what I want, I don't express opposition to them or convey anger through voice, atti-tude or body language. Instead, I request that they organise a meeting to discuss the issues that are causing problems for the company.

A meeting has been arranged for the next week, so I spend a lot of my time **preparing** for the meeting. I am aware that the only way I might get what I want will be if I make a convincing case about the benefits that the **company** will gain if I had an extra member of staff. The first thing that I will do is to make a list of all the benefits that the company will get by the Production Department having an extra staff member. Secondly, I make a list of all the objections that could be raised to my proposal. Thirdly, I will go through all the possible objections and see how I could deal with them.

Possible Objections

1. An extra employee would cost us too much.
2. We are in the process of restructuring the Production Department.
3. The person who left did not work well enough so there is no need to replace him or her.

I know **most** of the objections that will be raised and have a response prepared.

The next aspect of my preparation is to look at all the people who will decide on the issue that is being discussed and consider how **they** could benefit by my department having an extra employee. Here is where I become a **<u>SALESPERSON</u>**. I am **selling** my ideas and I am trying to convince other people to **buy** my ideas. When we look at sales people we see them selling products and services. However, selling **ideas** is no different. It is a similar system. Also we are dealing with human beings. If I was a salesperson in the motor industry and a person came into the garage and was looking at a car, **I** would want that person to buy that car because **I** would **benefit** from it. Being an **ineffective** salesperson I approach the customer and say, "Will you please buy this car? If you do **I** will get a 10% commission. Also the company has an award every summer for the "Sales Person of the Year" and if you buy this model **I** will have a good chance of becoming "Sales Person of the Year" which will mean that I will win the trip to Florida. I really want to achieve this." The potential buyer will be amazed at what I am saying. They will **not** buy that car and will leave the garage. They will then go to another garage to look at another vehicle. At this garage there is another salesperson who is also strongly committed to selling the car in order to earn a good commission and win an award. However, because the person is a very good "**salesperson**" they know that the customer will buy the car for the **benefits** that **they** will get. The salesperson will approach the customer and go through all the advantages that he or she will get by buying that vehicle. "This car will give you 50 miles to a gallon. It is very good on long journeys. The trade-in value in a few years will be very good. It does not rust for 10 years. It is very safe for children to travel in." All the advantages of the product and all the benefits that the buyer will get will be emphasised. The customer will be more likely to buy **that** car than the one that I was trying to sell, simply because of the approach adopted by the salesperson, who focussed on the benefits the customer would get by buying the car.

When I bought the computer system in my office it was not to make a profit for the computer company, but to assist **my** business. The reason why I took on a pension plan was to benefit **me** in years to come, not to make money for the insurance company. People who drink in a pub or eat in a restaurant do so because **they** enjoy the atmosphere, not because they want the owner to make money. I do not expect people to do business with companies in order to assist the companies. They buy products or services for personal reasons. As I say on my course to my participants, "The reason why you have come on my course is to develop **your** communication skills and become more confident and effective as an individual. You would not have said, 'Poor Frank, he needs the money, so I will do his course.' "

Going back to the meeting situation I will now outline how "Selling skills" can be used to persuade people to accept one's ideas. I am now in the process of preparing for my meeting so I am aware of all the people who will be attending the meeting and making the decision on my proposal to get an extra member in my department. As part of my preparation I am aware that most of the decision-makers will be influenced by how **they** would benefit from a more effective Production Department. In my mind I look at each person who will decide on what I want. John gets a report from me at the end of each month on the activities of my department. Due to the fact that I am working harder and longer I am not able to present the report as often as I used to. John is constantly contacting me requesting that I give him the report in order that he can do his work on time. I wish to do this, but I do not have the time to write the report. If I had an extra member in my department then I would have the time to prepare the report. That might influence John to support my proposal.

I also was involved in working on a project with Mary when I had time to do so. If I had an extra person in my department I would be able to revert back to assisting her. Kevin, a manager of another division, attends a meeting each week of the staff and I used to attend it a lot and make a good contribution to supporting him. Due to the pressure that I am having, I do not attend all the meetings and the ones that I do attend I have to leave early. If I had an extra member in my department I could attend the meetings and give support to him. As part of the preparation that I am doing, I have gone through all the benefits that the decision-makers will get from giving me what **I** want.

The meeting has now commenced and the chairperson says, "The next item on the agenda is the request by Frank to get another employee for his department." I now make my **PRESENTATION**.

"Thank you, Mr Chairman. As you are all aware Brian left the Production Department three months ago and he has not been replaced. This has had a negative effect on the entire company. Everyone here today has lost out because of that. The purpose of my proposal is to request you to consider replacing him as soon as possible in order that you will all benefit by the Production Department having an extra employee."

I did not say that **I** want you to give me what **I** want so that it will improve **my** situation. I then discussed all the benefits that would result across the whole company from giving me what I wanted.

"John, I am very aware of the problems that you are experiencing by not getting my report at the end of each month. If there was an extra employee in the Production Department then I would have more time to concentrate on writing the report and you will have it each month on the day that you require it.

"Mary, I would like to assist you as I have done in the past on the project that we worked on. If Brian is replaced soon, then I will have more time to devote to your project.

"Kevin, as you know I have supported you a lot at the meetings. Unfortunately, I have not been able to attend the meetings for too long due to the extra work that I am doing. If there was another person in my department then I would have more time to attend the meetings."

Throughout my presentation, I have not talked about what **I** want, but how the other people would benefit from giving me what **I** want; I am **selling** my proposal. This might win over some of the people to my proposal. However, it is possible that there will be some opposition to what I have said. The first point to consider is not to take an objection to one's ideas as an objection to one's self. Many people do take objections to what they are strongly committed to personally and this leads to the arguments and rows that occur at meetings.

Let's say that one or two people are opposed to my proposal and they outline their views on the issue. For me it would be unrealistic to expect everyone to agree with my views, thoughts and ideas. People can oppose each other on two basic principles. Firstly, they sincerely believe that the other person is wrong even though they are not opposed to the person as an individual. However, it can occur that because someone does not like another person that they will never agree with them on anything. If an individual is a good communicator they will be able to oppose someone, in a positive and constructive manner.

As I mentioned earlier, disagreement is not a bad thing and it can contribute to getting the right decision made. The effective communicator will help the individual to realise that they have made a mistake rather than pointing out how they made the mistake.

When a member of the committee is making a speech on why I should not get what I want, I will not interrupt them, abuse them, or tell them that they are wrong. Neither will I send signals through body language indicating that I am angry and that I am annoyed at what they are saying. I will sit authoritatively, listen to what is being said, and perhaps make a few notes. As part of the preparation that I did, I expected that this objection would be made and I have a response to it. When the people who have opposed my proposal have ended their talks, I can give the response that I prepared in a very diplomatic manner. If the people who oppose my proposal come across in a very negative way, I will not take it personally. I know that they are not effective in opposing people's ideas and that is **their** problem. They may be very good speakers with a good command of language but they are not good communicators due to the lack of knowledge of human behaviour.

The chairperson may now be unwilling to make a decision on my proposal and it is suggested that the issue will be raised again at the next meeting in three weeks time. Naturally, I would be disappointed that I did not get what I wanted, but I would not express that to the group. I would end by saying, "Thank you for discussing my proposal and I look forward to your decision at our next meeting." The meeting then comes to an end and the group all leave the room. Within a short time they might forget a lot of the points that I raised due to the busy situations that they are involved in. Over the next three weeks they may not spend any time considering how they will react to what I proposed. Three weeks later when I would walk into the meeting I would be very aware of all the issues that I discussed as it is to the forefront of my mind. The other people have their own situations that dominate them so I don't expect that they will all remember everything that I said.

To help me get what I want I will plan for the next meeting. A few days before it takes place I will send a letter or a fax to each participant and will place in bullet points the benefits that they will get from giving me what I want. This will bring back to the forefront of their minds all the points that I presented at the last meeting. That may help to convince them to give me what I want. This method would not be guaranteed to always achieve ultimate success but it works far better than going in to a meeting and telling people what they are to do, ordering them about and perhaps getting involved in arguments.

The final aspect that I wish to outline is how to reject another person's ideas in a constructive way. The incorrect way to oppose a person's ideas or proposals is to tell them that they are wrong and outline the potential pitfalls if they do what they propose. Most people do not like to be criticised and to have their ideas rejected and this can cause problems between people. For someone to say "No, that won't work, this will happen, that will happen" and go through all the things that could go wrong, can make the proposer feel that they are being treated as if they were stupid. Even though all people make mistakes and can be wrong in what they want to do, it is **wrong** to use that word to other people. The best way to handle this situation is to help the other person to see that they are wrong or that their ideas won't work.

The good communicator who is opposed to what someone has proposed would say something like: "Let us examine this proposal and see how it might work." To use the name of the proposer can help. "If we implement your proposal, Joan, could this happen?" And they say what they believe **could** happen. This will help the proposer to see that they perhaps did not research their idea as thoroughly as they might have done.

Another method would be, "If this was to happen, how do you think it could be dealt with?" Again it is helping the proposer to see the weakness in what they have projected without accusing them directly of making a mistake.

9

Negotiations

Negotiation is part of a person's life. All people have to negotiate, even though some people may not believe that they are negotiating. They would see negotiating as something that is done by people involved in national and international politics, industrial disputes, commercial mergers and take-overs. These get the headlines and that is why some people consider that negotiations only occur in the higher echelons of society. However, on a less exalted level, all human beings engage in this exercise with different degrees of skill and success. This chapter will outline what is meant by negotiation, the skills that a good negotiator must have, and will show how to develop these skills.

What are Negotiations?

The purpose of negotiations is to bring together all the interested parties in a conflict or disagreement, and to find a formula to narrow the difference that exists between them so that all sides can emerge satisfied that they have achieved success. Needless to say, compromises will have to be made, issues will have to be conceded, and tough bargaining should be expected. The fact that people agree to negotiate is an indication that they are interested in finding a solution to a problem. There is little point in entering negotiations if a party to them is not committed to resolving the differences that they have with other people. It is true, of course, that some people will agree to negotiate for appearance's sake and to pretend that they are serious about resolving the conflict. In such cases, their insecurity will be quickly exposed and they will probably do themselves more harm in the long run.

The skills of a good negotiator

The first thing to remember about negotiation is that one is dealing with people. A knowledge of human behaviour, an understanding of how people think, what motivates them, why they act and react as they do is essential. In the chapter on human behaviour I covered this aspect. The individual who has a good knowledge of human behaviour will be able to negotiate effectively. It is also helpful to remember that the people who solve the problems of the world are those who are tactful and diplomatic with the ability to bring people closer together. People who cause many of the conflicts tend to be those who shoot from the hip, who talk before they think, and who let emotions dictate their actions. The skilled negotiator will always be aware that the expression on one's face, the tone of voice used, and the choice of words will have a considerable bearing on the results that will be achieved. The following are some of the emotions that were referred to earlier and how they can affect negotiations.

Pride

As pride is part of the human condition, the skilled negotiator will endeavour to avoid situations where their opponents are backed into a corner, and where they may refuse to concede a point in case they lose face. No one likes to lose face, and even if they know that they are wrong the average person will feel obliged to adhere to their point regardless of the consequences. The skilled negotiator will let the other person save face. It is essential to keep the discussion focussed on the issues and not on the personalities involved.

Unfortunately, some negotiations descend to the level of each side attacking the other on a personal level, and this only exacerbates the problems and prolongs the discussions. Some people resent being criticised even though they are not slow to criticise others. If a person feels that they are being criticised, they tend to go on the defensive and attempt to justify what they have said or done.

In negotiations, it is important not to lay blame on the other side; even if they are clearly to blame. They will refuse to accept it and perhaps throw it back at those who proffered it. It is possible to make one's point strongly and to refute one's opponent's point without putting the other person down or applying any negative attributes to them.

So, the golden rules for negotiations are:

1. Not to get personal with the other side, even if they get personal.

2. Not to criticise or imply that one's opponent is wrong.

3. To try to let one's opponent save face.

Fear

It is useful to consider the personalities of the people who are on the other side of the table. Some people who take part in negotiations are not skilled in this field and may be vulnerable. They may be representing other people and are afraid that they will fail them. This is a pressure that negotiators may have to face. For the inexperienced negotiator to sit opposite a skilled one can be a daunting experience.

Signs that a member of the opposite side may be nervous could be as follows:

1. Excessive licking of their lips.

2. Hands clasped or fingers closely entwined.

3. Walking up and down the floor before the meeting starts.

4. Avoiding eye contact with those on the opposite side.

If the person is feeling nervous, they may misplay their hand or become excessively aggressive as they feel that this is the only way of handling a more experienced opponent.

Good verbal communication skills are very useful when negotiating. If a person does not have a good command of language and the ability to express themselves well, they can be intimidated by those who can argue their case with ease and effectiveness.

The fear of giving away too much is a fear that many inexperienced negotiators have, and it is one that is understandable. Deciding when is the appropriate time to make a concession, or concede a point, can be tricky.

Insecurity

Some people go through life feeling insecure in some aspect of their lives. For those taking part in negotiations, not having enough belief in themselves can be a problem. It comes down to self-confidence. A confident negotiator will have sufficient faith in his/her ability to conduct negotiations, and will not have to rely on gimmicks or ploys.

Ambition

In negotiations, individual ambitions can influence the approach of those taking part. A person who is trying to make a name for themselves may very well adopt a stance just to show their colleagues on the panel, or the members of the organisation involved, that they are strong, determined and uncompromising. Negotiations can be influenced by the fact that someone is manoeuvring for a position within their organisation or business. It is something that one has to live with. While each side to negotiations will have their own principles and objectives, individuals on all sides can have their own personal agenda.

The negotiation process

The following are the eight stages of the negotiation process:

1. Preparing for negotiations.

2. Opening the meeting.

3. Making the presentation.

4. Responding to the opposition.

5. Making proposals.

6. Signalling that compromises and changes are possible.

7. Bargaining.

8. Closing the meeting.

1. Preparing for the negotiations

In order to ensure that the meeting that will be held will be effective, spending time preparing for it is essential. While people who are taking part in meetings that deal with controversial issues may be emotional, it is essential not to allow one's feelings to influence one's behaviour at the meeting. The advantage of spending as much time as possible preparing for the negotiation session is that the individual will both feel and look more at ease when they start the discussions.

For example, assume someone was to meet with a group to negotiate on an issue and did not spend enough time preparing for the meeting. They walk into the room and see the people that they will be dealing with, sitting very comfortably, looking very relaxed and confident. That could make the individual feel uncomfortable because they believe that the other people are very well prepared for a discussion on the issues at hand. They are sending a signal that they will achieve what they want. When the other side see the person looking very nervous, they may be convinced that he/she is not well prepared and are receiving a sign that they are going to find the session difficult. If one is very well prepared, one will be able to walk into the room looking and feeling confident and in control, and this is very important.

How to prepare for negotiations

(a) Make a list of what is required: write down all of the things that one wants to achieve.

(b) Prioritise the issues: make a list of primary and secondary issues. The primary issues are the ones on which one is not willing to concede. The secondary issues are those that one can compromise on or concede at a later stage.

(c) Anticipate the objections that will be made and prepare a response to them: it is important to know most of the objections that could be raised against one's position and how to deal with them. One of the reasons why some people do not perform well in negotiations is that they are not prepared for some of the questions that are asked or issues that are raised by the other side.

In the chapter on meetings, more detailed information was given on how to anticipate objections that may be raised.

Awareness of the issues that will be raised at a negotiation session, and the knowledge and ability to deal with them, ultimately leads to relaxation, ease and confidence when walking into the room. The fourth stage of the preparation process is "researching the opposition". This means trying to find out as much as one can about the individual or group that one will be dealing with. For example, if a person was going to meet with another individual and they became aware of a problem that their opponent had, then they will be in a better position to handle the situation.

I learned that lesson many years ago when I was taking part in a negotiation session with a man who was opposing what I was doing in an organisation. When I discovered that he was going through a crisis with his wife, and he was in very bad form because of this, I decided that he would be more difficult to deal with than he would have been if he was not having that problem. Therefore, I expected that he would not perform well and that his attitude towards me would be influenced by his unfortunate situation. I was young at the time and had no experience in negotiations but when I learned that lesson, I became very pleased and that made me more effective in all the negotiations that I took part in.

To know that someone is unwell, or that they are having business problems, or that they are going through a crisis, will assist a negotiator to cope better with their opponent. While it may not be easy to find out what the temperament of one's opponent is, it is useful to spend as much time as possible investigating their situation.

In another negotiation session that I was involved in many years ago, I was meeting a panel of people in an organisation to discuss an issue. As part of the preparation that I made, I discovered that an election for the position of leader of the organisation would be taking place. That convinced me that the person who wanted to be made leader would be more difficult to deal with than some of the other people. He had his own agenda and would be committed to impressing the other members of his panel. Because I knew this, I was in a stronger position at the meeting.

Therefore, researching the opposition is an important stage of the preparation process.

The final stage of preparation is deciding when and how concessions can be made. As was outlined earlier, there are the two areas of primary and secondary issues. In relation to the secondary issues, it is important to know what would have to be given before a concession can be made. For example, if the opposition concede on a particular issue, then a concession can be made. Writing down what has got to be conceded by the other side and what can then be given in return is the most effective thing to do.

By taking note of these five stages of the preparation process, one will feel a lot more at ease and will be in a position to negotiate more effectively.

2. Opening

Before starting a negotiation session, it is useful to adopt the right attitude towards the people on the other side. When groups of people meet to negotiate, they will often be opposed to one another and may not have a lot in common. Different professions and industries have different cultures, and the people who are involved in them can be very committed to their own side. However, while there is a difference between many people, they are not members of a different species. They are all human beings, motivated by the various aspects of the human character that were outlined in the chapter on human behaviour.

It is important to see people as human beings first, and then by the occupation or culture to which they belong. For example, when a negotiation session takes place between management and unions, there is a considerable difference between both sides. They have different traditions and values, and are very committed to them. However, they are not a different species. They are all members of the human race and behave like human beings.

When political leaders from different countries meet to negotiate and sort out problems, there are differences between them due to the culture from which they come and the traditions to which they are committed. However, they are all members of the human race and have a great deal in common.

If people like and respect each other, then they will get on better and make more progress, even though there will be differences between them. In the past there were very long running industrial strikes. One of the reasons why things went on for so long was that both sides were totally opposed to each other. The majority of employers would have been opposed to the existence of trade unions and would have regarded them as "communists". The majority of union members would have been opposed to business people and would have regarded them as "capitalists", exploiting working people. The reason why there are not as many strikes now is that both sides seem to get on better. While there are still differences between them and they are strongly and genuinely committed to their position and standards, they do not seem to be as opposed to each other's existence, and are able to get together and discuss their differences in a cool and rational manner. I have done a lot of courses in companies and discovered that the personnel manager and the union representative had a good working relationship. They would not have a lot in common nor be socially friendly, but are able to meet and come to arrangements in an effective way. If the leaders of any two countries get on well together and like each other, it will improve relationships between both countries.

Therefore, in order to be an effective negotiator, it is essential that one is not strongly opposed to the rival faction, even though there will be differences on issues between both sides. If a negotiation starts off with both sides getting on well, then there is a good chance that progress will be made, even though there will be disagreements. If both sides are very negative towards each other, then that is a very bad start. If a person walks into the room and greets the individuals from the other side in a friendly way, using their names, that will contribute to a good start. If the last meeting ended badly with a row between both sides, or if one party abused another, then that could make it difficult for the second meeting to start in a friendly way.

As I outlined in the chapter on human behaviour, many people do not like to be criticised and may take what is said against them personally. Due to the fact that some people who negotiate are bad communicators, they will contribute to the other side not performing well when they meet again. It is understandable that a person could leave a meeting feeling upset and angry towards their opponent. However, it would help if they did not allow that to influence their attitude at the next meeting.

The more self-confident a person is, the easier it is for them to deal with difficult situations. Accepting that a person is not a good communicator and that they allow their feelings to influence their behaviour, is a good way of coping with difficult people. Over many years I have taken part in negotiations with people who spoke fluently, but to my knowledge, they were not good communicators. I never allowed them to upset me and I never took what they said as personal criticism. I would leave the meeting feeling grateful that I was not like them in how I dealt with people. When I would go into the next meeting, I would do so feeling at ease. Getting off to a good start is the first stage of the opening process.

The next stage is starting the meeting in a constructive manner. Once again the tone of voice, eye contact, facial expression and body language will have a role to play. Another aspect is the choice of words. Using the right words to deal with the issues is essential.

When both sides enter negotiations, they want to win and get the best result for themselves or their organisations. While that is understandable, it usually ends with compromises and concessions being made, leading ultimately to a negotiated settlement. Most people do not like to be told or ordered to do something. They would like to feel that they agreed to accept a position, not that they were forced into it. In the chapter on meetings, I outlined how to persuade and influence people to accept one's ideas and how to oppose people in a constructive manner.

Opening the negotiation session in a positive and constructive way will contribute to progress being made and both sides being able to achieve some of the things they want. When negotiations take place between two groups, it is ideal to have a neutral chairperson who will contribute to both sides making progress. If there is no chairperson, then both sides should regard each other as equal and not see themselves as the definitive group.

3. Making presentations

In the chapter on presentations, I will outline that making a presentation is not just standing up to speak to a group with an overhead projector. Sitting around a table at a negotiation session is a form of presentation.

The first aspect of making a good presentation is maintaining eye contact with the people on the other side. To spend too much time staring up and down will not establish a good rapport with one's opponents. While one may have to read a certain amount, it is essential not to ignore the other people. Looking at all the people and doing so in a pleasant way will improve the atmosphere.

Using one's hands in the right fashion will also contribute to a conducive atmosphere. To have a pen in one's hand and to point it to the other side can be interpreted by them as a form of aggression. Aiming one's hands across the table can also be interpreted as a form of aggression. To use one's hands to emphasise points and to enliven the delivery is acceptable. Sitting authoritatively at a negotiation session is similar to standing authoritatively when giving a speech. To be bent over the table and looking uncomfortable will not be a good way to present one's case.

To speak clearly and make a lively delivery will contribute to getting one's point across without ambiguity, or misinterpretation. The tone of voice that is used is important. When a person is speaking, the way that they hear what is being said can differ from how the listeners hear it. While it is important to make a lively delivery, it is equally vital not to be seen to shout or talk too hard, as this will be interpreted as a form of aggression. To maintain the right facial expression is also essential. Once again, like the speaking voice, it is difficult to know how one is looking unless there is a mirror in front. To be seen to be unpleasant, angry, with a face twisting too much can also be seen as negative.

The final aspect of making a good presentation when negotiating is the choice of words that are used. The use of some words can be misinterpreted. Using words like "never" tends to do two things:

(a) It leads the opposition to respond in a particular manner, often negatively.

(b) It can make it difficult for the negotiator to concede on the point in question at a later stage.

"We will never agree to. . . ."

"We will never accept this. . . ."

As the negotiations proceed, the issue may turn out to be less objectionable, but having used the word "never", it can be more difficult to concede as this will be seen as losing face.

Using a word like "don't" can also be misinterpreted. To use it in relation to one's own situation is acceptable:

"I don't object to what you want me to consider."

"I don't mind your objection to my proposal."

"I don't mind us not sorting out this issue at this meeting."

However, to say:

"I don't want to do. . . ."

"I don't want to accept your suggestion on. . . ."

"I don't think you are right to suggest. . . ."

could be misinterpreted.

Another word that can cause a difficulty is "wrong". To admit that oneself was wrong to do or say something is all right, but to tell the opposing faction that they were "wrong" will have a negative effect. "Object" is another word that could get a negative response. Using it to comment on one's own reaction could work, if used in the following way:

"I would not object to your suggestion on. . . ."

"I might accept your objection to. . . ."

To say "I will object to what you want me to do" will get a negative reaction. "Oppose" can have a similar effect:

"I would not oppose your views on . . ." would be acceptable.

"I will strongly oppose what you want to change in this . . ." will be more difficult. In the section on making proposals, the use of appropriate words that will help to get a good reaction will be outlined.

The key features when making a good presentation of points in a negotiation are as follows:

a) maintain good eye contact with the people that one is addressing

b) keep one's hands under control and to use them just to emphasise points

c) sit authoritatively

d) speak clearly with the right tone of voice

e) maintain good facial expression

f) use the right words

4. Responding to one's opponent

When the first group have ended their presentation, the opposite side will commence their presentation. Because both sides are opposed to each other, what can happen is that when the second side starts talking their opponents will react negatively, either verbally or physically. One of the most important skills in negotiations is not just talking, but listening.

When the opposition is making their opening presentation, it is essential to listen and never interrupt. Even if things are being said that will cause concern, it is still useful to let them keep talking until they finish. When their arguments have to be refuted, it is important to avoid using phrases which will aggravate them. Such comments might be:

"You can't be serious!"

"That is the greatest rubbish that I have ever heard!"

"What kind of fools do you think we are?"

This type of reaction will provoke the other side and negate what is supposed to be achieved, *i.e.* finding common ground.

When both sides have made their opening presentation, the way is now clear for the next phase – "Arguing". This word has a negative connotation. However, real argumentation is discussing and this is the main aspect of the negotiation process. Each side will present their ideas and will want to persuade their opponents to accept them. The following are the best ways of responding to one's opponent.

(a) Listening

Listening intently to what is being said and avoiding interrupting.

(b) Avoiding Point Scoring

It is best to avoid point scoring. This means outlining to people what they have done wrong and proving that they have made mistakes. Even if someone has given their opponent an opportunity to make an issue of what they have said that was wrong, it is better not to try to show the person that they are ineffective or lacking.

(c) Avoiding Attacking People

If a person says something that is outrageous, a blatant lie, or is insulting, it is understandable that one may want to hit out at them. Resisting the temptation to attack and asking them to withdraw their comment in a cool and constructive manner will be more successful.

(d) Avoiding Blaming People

Blaming the other side for what has gone wrong will not achieve a great deal. No one likes to be blamed for anything, even if they are in the wrong.

(e) Not Being too Clever

To be seen to be too clever does not enhance one's negotiating position. Sometimes an occasion will occur where the temptation will be there to show off how smart one thinks one is. Avoiding this trap contributes to a better atmosphere all round.

(f) Not Talking too much

Try to avoid talking too much. Listening is a very important part of all communication, and this applies to negotiation as much as any other aspect of contact between people. It is especially important not to shout one's opponent down. Some negotiators feel that threats, abuse, sarcasm or bullying is necessary in order to gain the upper hand. All it does, however, is alienate further those one is negotiating with, thereby making agreement more difficult.

5. Making proposals

Each side in the negotiation sessions will try to convince the other to accept their ideas. While some people are willing to accept someone else's views or recommendations, others can react negatively. To tell people what they must do and why they must do it can provoke a negative reaction, even if it is a good idea and will be of benefit to sorting out a problem. The most effective way to get a positive reaction from one's opponent is to "make suggestions". Ask them to "consider" what one wants them to do. Many people like to have their advice sought on issues and to feel that they contributed to finding a solution. To say, "Would you be willing to consider making this change?" would be far more effective than saying, "I want you to accept this change".

It is a good idea to say things like, "What would your reaction be to (outline point)?", "Do you think that this (outline point) will be worth implementing?", "Would you be in favour of (outline point)". While there is no easy way to get people to abandon their own ideas and to accept those of their opponents, making proposals in the manner outlined is more effective than telling people what to do and trying to force them to accept one's recommendations. In the chapter on meetings, how to reject other people's ideas is outlined [see page 73].

When I first took part in negotiation sessions in the late 1960s, I made mistakes. I felt strongly about what I wanted and tried to convince my opponents to accept what I wanted them to do in a negative way. I told them what to do and why to do it. They behaved in the same way towards me and this led to the meetings ending with no agreement. An issue that was being discussed was causing a problem due to the fact that we both had several meetings to deal with it and no progress was made. When one of the meetings ended it did so in a negative way and I then realised that if progress was to be made, that I would have to change the way that I was performing.

A week later we met again and I greeted my opponents and said, "Hopefully we can narrow the differences between us on this issue at today's meeting."

This got a good reaction and some of the people smiled at me. I then said, "Would you be willing to consider this..." and gave an outline of what I wanted.

"Yes, Frank. We will consider it," one man said.

I then asked them for their views on the issues. I made suggestions and while I did not get everything that I wanted, I did get a settlement that was acceptable to me, as did the other side. Making proposals in the manner outlined will contribute to progress being made.

6. Signalling

When the time has come to concede or compromise, it is useful to send a signal to the other side that one is prepared to do so. The words that can be used to send signals are as follows:

"all"
"at present"
"most"
"as things stand"

For example:

"I cannot accept all the things that you want me to" is a signal that one is willing to accept some of them.

"It would be too difficult at present to make this change" is a signal that it might be possible to do so later.

"Most of what you have outlined is interesting" is a signal that while one is not in favour of all of what was presented, it is possible that some things will be accepted.

"As things stand I don't think that we should do ....." is a signal that if things change, then it will be possible to accept what was proposed.

When people are going to buy a product or service, they will send what is called a "buying signal". The experienced salesperson is able to identify the signal and this leads them to the closing stage. In order to hear the signal that is being sent, it is essential to listen while the other person is talking. As I outlined in the chapter on conversation, some people are not listening to what is being said and are thinking of what they will say in response. When negotiations are taking place between two groups, it is useful for one person on each panel to act as a listener for signals.

In the late 1970s, I was part of a panel of three people who were taking part in negotiations. I did not do much talking. I thought that a signal might be sent from the other side that a compromise would be considered. I listened and when someone said, "As things stand we could not agree with this", my two colleagues were too busy thinking what to say next to hear what had been said. I heard what was said and wrote a note, stating "He has said that he won't agree with our proposal, as things stand. That might mean that they will agree later if we discuss it in more detail." My colleagues then became aware of what was said and that improved the situation. Therefore, sending signals that one is willing to consider something else and listening to the signals that are being sent has a role to play in negotiations.

7. Bargaining

Most of time in the negotiation process is spent on the area of bargaining. This is where both sides are trying to get the best deal for themselves. Many of the areas that have been outlined will take place in this section: presenting ideas, responding to reactions, making proposals, signalling that concessions will be made.

No one wants to concede on any point without getting something back in return. An effective way to achieve this is to use the word "if". That word has an important role to play in negotiations. For example, "If you agree to . . ., I will be willing to agree to . . .". That is letting the other side know what changes one is willing to accept, and under what circumstances.

Another aspect of the bargaining section is presenting packages. As part of the preparation, it is useful to put together a package and decide when to present it. While bargaining could be seen as just one of the eight stages in the negotiation process, it is the main stage, and the longest one.

8. Closing

When the negotiations have come to an end, it is essential to close the meeting in a constructive way. The first thing to consider is whether there will be another meeting in the future between both sides on a different issue. If there will, it will be to the benefit of everyone to end the meeting with both sides on good terms with each other. If both sides leave the room in good form, pleased that they have got on well together and satisfied that they have achieved some of the things they wanted, then it will be easier for them to meet in the future. However, if the meeting ends with both sides angry with each other, and feeling negative towards each other, then the next time that they have to meet, both sides will be more likely to have negative feelings towards each other. This can contribute to a difficult start.

It is very useful to remind people what they have achieved and what concessions one has made. If the negotiations took place over a long period and concessions were made at early meetings, then while the other side would have been pleased at the time when they got concessions, they may have come to take them for granted after such a long time. To remind one's opponent that one was opposed to something but that a concession was made to their benefit, will contribute to establishing a good rapport with the other side. When people become aware of what they have achieved, it can convince them to terminate the negotiations.

After the meeting comes to an end, it is useful to thank the other side for taking part in the negotiations and to express gratitude for the concessions that they made. It is also essential to apologise for any negative things that one may have done or said. This will contribute to both sides leaving the meeting in a more positive frame of mind.

There are times when agreement is not possible and deadlock occurs and this entails both sides going back to the drawing board. However, if good communication skills and diplomacy are used throughout the discussions, this will contribute to success.

10

Presentations

When most people think of the word "presentation" they picture some-one standing up before a group with an overhead projector. This is of course true but presentation should not be seen in such a narrow con-text. When people attend a meeting they are presenting. When they take part in an interview or participate at appraisals, they are making a presentation. Going to a bank to borrow money for business or per-sonal reasons is part of the presentation process. Even meeting an indi-vidual to discuss an issue or raise a matter is a form of presentation.

Public speaking and presentation skills

When I set up my business it was to train people in "public speaking" (it is now called "presentation skills".) At that time most private citi-zens did not have to stand up and speak to groups. There were a few occasions when men had to perform in public. In the old days, only men had to do a lot of things. A man would be at a wedding, giving his daughter away, being the best man, or as the groom. Some belonged to residents' associations, sports groups, and other organisations.

The first point to make about most people who have to stand up and speak to groups is that the majority of them suffer from an element of fear. Fear is part of the human condition, and most people have differ-ent types of fears. My greatest fear is heights. To stand up on the roof of a tall building can make me feel uncomfortable. Other people have a fear of flying – going up in a plane is an ordeal; going across the sea in a boat; very open or enclosed spaces; fear of animals, dogs, cats, or things like mice and rats. These are what are called phobias. Most are just an inconvenience. However, if a person has a fear of standing up and speaking to groups and then they get a position or are appointed to a committee where addressing groups is part of their brief, this can be a very difficult situation.

I have heard from time to time that people's fear of speaking in public is greater than the fear of death, the fear of illness, losing a mem-ber of one's family, or losing one's job. I disagree with this. While speaking in public can be a daunting and very frightening experience for some, I find it hard to accept that it is more terrifying than losing one's life or one's partner, children or career. The great fear that most people have about standing up before a group is the fear of making a fool of themselves. The fear of going blank in the middle of a talk and letting oneself down in front of other people. That is perfectly understandable. No one likes the idea of humiliating themselves in public. There is however, a difference between being apprehensive about speaking and being fearful of speaking. Most people who perform in public experience a level of tension just before they start. Many well-known actors, singers and entertainers have admitted that sometimes they feel nervous just before they walk on stage, especially on a first night. This is natural and one should not be put off by a degree of nerves or tension. In many ways it can be a positive thing as it keeps people in control. It is the adrenaline in action.

The reason why so many people have taken part in my public speaking course is that they are ordinary, private citizens. If a person is well-known, or has a position of considerable status, then it is easier for them to stand up and make an impact in front of an audience. Many people are impressed by well-known individuals and like to hear what they have to say. If someone is a politician, a leading clergyman, an actor, singer, musician, sportsperson, broadcaster or journalist, then it is a lot easier for him or her to stand up and speak.

The nerves normally come as the Chairperson is introducing the speaker. That is when the speaker can get "the butterflies in the tummy". There is a well-known saying that one can never get rid of the butterflies; it is a question of teaching them to fly in formation.

The level of apprehension that a speaker has will be influenced by five main factors:

1. Knowledge of the Subject

If the speaker is very knowledgeable on the topic that they are speaking on, then they will feel a lot more comfortable than if they are dealing with material that is new to them or that they have not researched in detail.

2. The Level of Preparation

A speaker could be very knowledgeable on the subject but if they have not prepared their talk, or structured it to suit the audience, this will make them less confident and more nervous.

3. The Composition of the Audience

The composition of the audience can determine the level of fear or apprehension that the speaker experiences.

(a) If an employee of a company was making a presentation to a group that included the Chairperson of the Board, the Chief Executive, and senior managers this might make them a lot more nervous than if they were talking to a group that did not include people at that level. Most human beings like to make a good impression to their higher executives and would not like to let themselves down in front of them.

(b) A person making a business presentation that could result in them getting a large contract could feel more ill at ease because the stakes are very high and the success of the presentation will contribute to them getting the contract.

(c) An individual representing an important or prestigious organisation can be less comfortable when speaking as they will be conscious that if they do not do well they will let their organisation down before the audience.

(d) A manager making a presentation to members of his or her staff could feel that if they went blank or made a bad presentation, their employees would have seen a weakness in them and this could lower their prestige and standing in the eyes of their staff.

(e) If a member of the audience is more knowledgeable on the subject than the person who is speaking. Years ago a young man who attended my course told me a story. He was in the computer industry and gave courses in computer skills. He never found it a problem and he enjoyed giving the courses. One morning, before the course started, he got involved in a conversation with a girl who was taking part in the programme. From the conversation it transpired that she knew a lot about computers. The reason she was there was that there was an elderly man attending with her. Their company had installed a new system and they wanted this man to go on a course. He was reluctant to do so as he felt that all the participants would be very young and he would be out of his depth. Also he thought that he was too old to start learning about computers. However, the company wanted him to go, so this girl suggested that she would accompany him and give him support.

The young man who was the trainer told me: "When I give my courses I do make the odd mistake here and there. But all the participants know nothing about computers so no one can make an issue of it. However, on that day I knew there was somebody who knew a lot about computers and that they would be aware of any little error that I might make. I was less comfortable presenting that course than I normally am."

That is very understandable and lots of people will experience that situation. If the person making the speech was to walk into the room and saw an individual who was known to be very knowledgeable on the topic that was to be covered, the speaker could feel uncomfortable.

4. The Venue

A person could be very relaxed making a presentation in a venue that they felt comfortable in. Yet if they had to move to a different venue they could feel more ill at ease.

Some years ago a man did my course and he told me this story. He is in the advertising industry and regularly gave presentations to clients in his office which is a Georgian building in Dublin. He never had any difficulty speaking to groups. One day he was asked to address a meeting in the Royal Hospital in Kilmainham. He prepared his talk very well and arrived at the venue. When he walked in the door and saw the size of the room he suddenly felt uncomfortable. "I never find it a problem speaking in my own office but I felt more nervous speaking in such a big hall," he said. That is understandable, as it is natural to feel more at ease in a venue that one is familiar with.

5. The Occasion

An occasion that is very formal and prestigious with important figures in attendance can make a speaker feel less comfortable than an informal gathering with people casually dressed and looking relaxed. An occasion that is confrontational can make the speaker more uneasy than a friendly, social gathering.

Checklist:

The five main areas that can determine the level of the speaker's confidence are:

1. The speaker's knowledge of the subject.

2. The level of preparation that they have done.

3. The composition of the audience.

4. The venue that they are speaking in.

5. The occasion at which they are speaking.

Overcoming the fear of public speaking

Overcoming the fear of speaking to groups and controlling tension and nerves has to be the first priority of those who have to make presentations. There are four main ways that this can be achieved:

1. Preparing thoroughly.

2. Knowing what to do if things go wrong.

3. Having the ability to think on one's feet.

4. Having plenty of practice and experience of speaking to groups.

Of these, by far the most important is thorough preparation.

Preparation

A speaker who is well prepared not only feels more confident, they also look more confident and usually make more interesting talks. To have to sit and listen to someone who has not prepared their talk well can be very unpleasant and it reduces the status not only of the speaker but also possibly of the content of the presentation.

The reason why many people do not prepare adequately is due to the pressures that they have to contend with. Business pressures, personal issues, the need to relax and forget about things. Most people intend to devote time to preparing a talk but it is often looked upon as a long-term priority as other issues take precedence. Then the speaker suddenly realises that the presentation is only days away and they can get very uneasy and wish that they had spent more time preparing. All human beings are risk takers to some extent; this is part of the human condition. One of the greatest risks that people take is standing up to speak without having spent sufficient time preparing and structuring their talk. Spending as much time as possible preparing is the first step in overcoming one's fear of speaking.

One of the problems that people can experience when they start preparing is getting writer's block. They sit down with a pen and a piece of paper, write down the title and then stop. Before putting pen to paper there are a number of questions that should be addressed.

(a) Who are my audience?

It is essential to know as much as possible about the group that one will be addressing. How many people will be in attendance and how knowledgeable they will be on the topic on which one is speaking, are key questions. Some people prepare a standard talk and deliver it to all the groups that they address. I would not recommend this, as each audience will be different. It is essential to pitch a presentation to suit the specific audience. For example, when a group is very knowledgeable on the subject on which one is speaking, it is acceptable to use technical terms or jargon and this will be fully understood by all in attendance. However, if the audience is composed of people who are not experts on the topic, then it is important to pitch it at a level that they will be able to understand, and explain any unfamiliar terms clearly. A mistake that some speakers make is that they assume that because they are very knowledgeable on the subject, those who are listening will have no difficulty in understanding what they are saying.

In the mid 1970s I attended a meeting which was being addressed by an expert in the area of finance. He was speaking to a mixed group about financial matters. He was a very good speaker, lively, enthusiastic, and witty. However, he made one big mistake. He forgot that there were people like me in the audience who were not very knowledgeable on the intricate details of financial matters. He started using some technical terms and initials that those from the banking, insurance or accountancy professions would have fully understood. But to those of us who were out of our depth when it came to detailed technical terminology, it was difficult for us to understand what was being outlined.

Having a reception with some people after the meeting I heard them saying that they were unsure of what he meant on a number of issues. That speaker who was trying to influence the audience to make investments possibly lost some potential clients due to talking over our heads.

Before starting to write or structure a talk, it is a good idea to try to find out as much as possible about the nature of the audience.

(b) What is the purpose of the presentation?

The second aspect of good presentation is knowing exactly what one wants to convey to those who will be listening. This can be done by making a list of all the issues that one wants to cover, then putting the list in the most appropriate sequence. A useful question to consider is, "How many of the points that will be covered will be remembered by the audience?" The more points that a speaker deals with, the greater the risk that some will be forgotten by the audience. The ideal situation is that the entire audience should be able to leave the room remembering everything that was covered by the speaker. In order to achieve this, it helps to keep the number of points as low as possible.

If it is necessary to deal with a lot of issues, then the best way to ensure that all will be retained is to give a set of notes to the audience, outlining the aspects that were covered in the talk. If notes are to be given, they should only be given at the end of the presentation, in order to stop the audience reading the notes while the speaker is talking.

(c) What will be the appropriate length of the presentation?

Deciding the length of time that would be appropriate for the presentation is the next stage of the preparation process. When doing this it is always useful to think about the people who will be listening in order to ensure that they will find the talk interesting and will not let their minds wander after a period. It is essential to remember that the onus is on the speaker to hold the interest of the audience and to convey what they want to say without ambiguity or misinterpretation. The longer the talk goes on, the greater the risk that those listening will lose interest, and may miss important points that the speaker wants to emphasise.

The ideal length of time to hold an audience's attention is about twenty minutes. However, there are occasions when the speaker has to go on longer in order to cover what they want to convey. If this should happen, it is important to structure the presentation in order to get the audience involved. If people are involved, they will pay more attention to what is being said, find the talk more interesting and retain more of the information. The following example should show the importance of organising and structuring time when speaking.

Since 1984 I have been the consultant to the Institute of Chartered Accountants in Ireland, in the area of presentation skills. Years ago, I got a call from a leading accountancy practice that was experiencing a difficult situation. They had organised a series of six meetings dealing with an aspect of finance for groups of people from the business world. They asked a senior member of the practice, a very experienced person in the area, to conduct the sessions.

He prepared his material well in terms of content and arrived at the hotel at 6.00 p.m. on the first night. Coffee, tea and sandwiches were served to the guests and at 6.30 p.m. they all entered the room where the meeting was to take place. At 6.35 p.m. the speaker stood up and started his presentation. He continued to speak until ten minutes to eight, reading from notes in a voice that was low and monotone. After about twenty minutes some members of the audience began to lose interest and some at the back of the room were quietly conversing with each other; one was doing a crossword and two others slipped out the door. When the speaker ended at ten to eight, he got a short round of applause and the group all ran out of the room, many of them heading for the bar.

The speaker, who we will call Jack, went into the men's room and was drying his hands on the towel. His back was to the door and three men entered and were discussing the presentation. They did not recognise Jack as his back was to them and one was saying,

"An hour-and-a-half he went on! Wouldn't you expect that they would have sent somebody more professional?"

A second man said "Yes. He had a very dull voice."

Suddenly Jack realised, "They are talking about me!" and he ran into a cubicle and closed the door, but it was still possible to hear people talking.

"I hope he is not on next week," one of the men said.

"I'm not coming if he is!" replied another.

"I wonder if I could get a refund?" asked the other.

Jack became very upset, to the extent that he actually vomited listening to the three men discussing his presentation. I am sure that had they recognised him, they would not have continued their conversation, but would have done so over a drink in the bar. Jack was reluctant to leave the toilet and he sat there for about twenty minutes. Then he opened the door and ran out. He left the hotel and went home feeling devastated.

Two days later, the Managing Partner heard about the experience and called Jack up to his office.

"I believe things didn't go well on Tuesday, Jack," he said.

"No," said Jack. "They didn't like me."

"Well maybe next week's group will be more responsive," said the Managing Partner.

"I'm not doing it next week," said Jack.

"But you have to!" said the partner. "You're our leading expert in this area!" "I really don't want to give more talks," said Jack.

The Managing Partner became concerned as the event had been arranged for the next five weeks and they did not have anyone available to replace Jack. He contacted me and I made an appointment to meet Jack.

"I would like to ask you Jack, why things did not go so well?"

"I don't know," he replied.

"I believe that you spoke for about an hour and a quarter?" I said.

"Yes." Jack replied. "I had to cover a lot of information. I could not have done it in a shorter time."

"I understand," I said. "However, if you would like to do it again next week, you might consider doing it this way."

"I'm not going to do it again," Jack said to me.

"I appreciate that," I said. "Let's say if you had done it this way. I accept that it was very good to have a reception before the talk started. However, because your session had to go on for so long, the listeners should have had another break. While students are able to sit and listen to lecturers or teachers for a long time, many people attending presentations given by private citizens like me or you would not like to listen for too long.

" You could have spoken for twenty, or twenty-five minutes, on the issues that you knew were the most important. Then you could have organised a question-and-answer session, having arranged with one of your colleagues to ask the first question to help get the process going. You see, many of the audience would like to have been involved and you could have conveyed a lot of information through a question-and-answer session. Then you could have given the group another fifteen-minute break.

"After the break you could have set up a project for the audience to work on. There were twenty-five people in attendance, so a certain number could have been placed around all the tables that were in the room. Each group could have been given an issue to go through in detail. All you would have had to do was to go around each group and outline what you wanted them to do and give them advice. After a period of time an individual from each group could give an outline on what they had learned. You could then stand up and give a brief summary."

He then looked at me and asked,

"Would that work?"

"Yes, Jack," I said. "It would work a lot better than reading for as long as you did. If you would like to consider doing it next week, I will attend with you and in the interim we can meet to plan and structure the event."

He agreed, and I met him for a number of sessions and did some work on his voice in order to make it easier to listen to.

Arriving at the hotel on the following Tuesday, he looked a bit nervous but as he was well prepared and had structured his presentation to suit the time that he had to speak, he was feeling a lot better than when he last stood on those steps. He started by introducing himself and his practice and outlined how the session would be held. This attracted the interest of the audience, as they knew that they would be participating rather than just listening. He spoke for twenty minutes and his voice was more lively. He then opened the meeting to the audience and this generated a great deal of discussion. A lot of interesting questions were asked and he conveyed his information in this way.

After twenty minutes of questions and answers, he invited the audience to join him for a break which lasted for fifteen minutes. I noticed as he spoke to some of the people that he looked very relaxed and at ease. He then brought the audience back and put them into groups of five and set a project for each group. He walked around giving ideas and advice, and was looking very comfortable. After about half an hour of discussion in the groups, he called upon an individual from each section to give their views on the project that they had discussed. When this ended, he stood up and for about ten minutes gave a summary. He got a good round of applause and as the people left the room, many went up to shake his hand and to express their gratitude for what they had learned.

Jack was very pleased and he invited me for a meal and said to me,

"You know, I never realised how important it was to structure a talk and to consider the idea of time."

The next week he attended on his own and at the end of the meeting he told a joke and got a very good reaction. He now regularly gives presentations and finds them no problem.

So if you ever have to make a presentation or give a speech that has to go on for a long time, always think about the people in the audience and try to structure it in some way to get them involved.

Another area where time becomes an issue is the order in which one is speaking. If a person is taking part in a seminar, a conference or a workshop and they are the first speaker of the day, then they have an advantage. For example:

It is 9.30 a.m. and the audience is bright and alert and looking forward to an interesting day. By late afternoon they have been listening to several speakers, have taken in a lot of information, have had a lunch and maybe something to drink. They are now getting a little tired and may be anxious to leave. The speaker who is selected to make the final presentation has a more difficult task than those who spoke earlier.

The way to deal with this matter is for the speaker to glance around the audience and look for signs that people emit when they may be getting bored. As well as the usual ones like yawning, there may be people speaking to the person beside them, reading through the notes of the previous speaker, looking at the paintings on the walls, counting the number of dots on the ceiling, looking at their watches, or, worse still, removing their watches and shaking them. This is a strong signal that some members of the audience are getting tired and want the meeting to end. The good speaker will recognise the signs and in order to keep the interest of the audience will decide to shorten their talk and tell the audience why they are doing it.

Years ago I was in that situation. I was taking part in a conference and was selected to give the last talk of the day. I was to speak from a quarter to five until five-thirty. Because I was to be the last speaker I got the impression that many members of the audience might not want to hear me talk for so long. I decided to look around for the signals that might be sent indicating that the listeners would prefer to be let out. I decided to reduce my talk and I would inform the listeners that they would be given a set of notes covering all the areas that I would have spoken on.

It was a very hot day in May and the room was getting very warm. The person who was speaking before me was getting a negative reaction. Lots of people were talking to each other and reading the notes that they were given at the lunch break. When the chairperson introduced me, I started my speech by saying:

"As you will see from the programme, I am supposed to speak until five-thirty. I appreciate that you have had a very interesting day and that you have benefited from all the speakers. However, it is very hot here and I am sure that you would like to leave soon. I have decided to reduce my talk and to give you all a set of notes on the issues that I wish to cover, so that you will benefit from my talk as you have from the other speakers."

I got a very strong round of applause and many people shook themselves and sat up in their seats. I went on for half an hour and spoke in a lively way so that the audience would not lose interest. I did eliminate some of the points that I believed were least important in order to reduce the time that I spent talking. However, the audience would have been able to get all the information due to the fact that they got notes on the issues that I decided not to speak on. The response from the audience was very positive.

These are two areas where timing is very important. As part of the preparation one should always pay special attention to time.

(d) How shall I begin my presentation?

The next stage in the preparation process is to decide on an opening that will hold the attention of the listeners. There are three potential openings that I would recommend depending on the occasion or the topic.

The first is a preamble, where the speaker outlines the areas that will be covered in the talk. If I were giving a talk on presentations, I would use the following opening:

"Good evening, ladies and gentlemen. I am going to speak to you this evening on how to make effective presentations. I am going to deal with the following areas:

"How to structure and prepare a presentation.

"How to deliver a presentation in a lively manner.

"How to use notes and visual aids.

"How to generate a response from the audience.

"How to deal with difficult questions or opposition to your ideas.

"When I have dealt with these issues I will invite you to put any questions that you may wish to discuss."

That is a simple method of opening a talk as it gives the audience a clear idea as to what the speaker is going to deal with. Having given an outline of the main areas that will be covered, one can then go into detail on each issue.

A second opening would be a question to the audience. This can be very effective as most people will begin to consider their response so the speaker has the majority of the audience focused on the issue that will be covered:

"How many people have ever heard of. . . . ?"

"Hands up all those who would be in favour of. . . . ?"

There is one risk in asking a question and that is if the response from the audience is negative or indifferent, as this can make the speaker feel uneasy.

The third way to make an opening is to give a quotation, or tell a story.

The main point is to get the audience interested at this early stage, in what is going to be covered.

I always recommend that one should avoid using clichés. Any phrase that is used too often becomes a cliché and subsequently loses its impact and effect.

Many people who have not trained in giving talks tend to use an opening that they have heard other people using. The fact that the people who use it are well known or have prestigious positions impresses some people. As I said in the opening chapter, well-known or prestigious people are not experts in everything.

Some of the clichés that people use at an event are: "It gives me great pleasure", or "I am delighted to be here." These phrases were used by Mr. Gottlieb in the great Marx Brothers' comedy, "A Night at the Opera." While they are not dreadful things to say, they are clichés.

I would address a group at an event as follows:

"Good evening, ladies and gentlemen. Thank you for coming to (Name of Event). I would like to firstly extend my gratitude to (Name of Sponsor) for the great support that they have given to our organisation."

I would then name someone who is senior in the company and thank them. Then I would thank other people who are involved and have contributed to the event. Finally, to wish the audience well and hope that they enjoy the event.

If members of the audience are important people, such as a government ministers, ambassadors, or leading Churchmen, then it is useful to address them firstly.

Notes, visual aids, equipment

The next stage of preparation is organising the notes that will be used, arranging visual aids such as acetates and slides, and examining any equipment that will be used.

Notes

Notes can either enhance or undermine a presentation or talk. The type of notes that I do not recommend using are sheets of paper with the content written in full and read word for word. That is more like an essay. Essays are meant to be read; talks are meant to be listened to. To stand up before a group and read a talk is one certain way of losing the interest of an audience. The speaker will tend not to maintain eye contact with the listeners which is essential to keep their attention. There are however occasions when it may be necessary to read in order to make a particular statement and use every word that the speaker has to mention. In the section on "Delivery," how to do this will be outlined in detail.

Another thing to avoid is memorising a talk word for word. That can sound more like a recitation. Let's say I am going to give a talk on the topic of censorship. I have prepared it word for word. I did it to the mirror before I left the house and everything is looking good. I stand up and say, "Good evening, ladies and gentlemen. Tonight I am going to talk to you on the topic of censorship.

"As you are aware, censorship in Ireland has always been a very controversial topic and many great works of art were banned for reasons that most people nowadays would find totally unacceptable.

"However, even the most liberal amongst us would be concerned about. . . . BLANK. Even the most liberal amongst us would be concerned about. . . . BLANK."

I have now forgotten the next word and that is the link to the rest of the content, so I am going to feel very uneasy.

The best way to avoid something like this happening is to use a set of notes. The ideal way to use notes is to have a number of small cards. Paper can quiver unless it is placed on a lectern and this can give a signal to the audience that the speaker is nervous. Cards don't quiver as easily and they can be held more comfortably than A4 sheets of paper. The purpose of the cards is to remind the speaker of the sequence of the points that are going to be dealt with. This will avoid them missing points or raising them in the wrong order.

This time I am going to give my talk on the topic of censorship with the aid of cards, using a number of small-sized cards, with the following points:

1. Introduction – Purpose of talk.

2. History of censorship.

3. Effects of censorship.

4. How things changed.

5. Conclusion.

Visual Aids

Most people who make presentations use an overhead projector or a slide projector.

Equipment

When using an overhead or slide projector, a microphone or showing a video it is important to examine the equipment before the presentation starts. The reason for this is that while all of these may look alike, they do vary in terms of how they operate. While most overhead projectors look similar, there are small differences in where the on/off buttons are placed, and in how to arrange the focus or deal with the light going off. As part of the preparation for a talk, the speaker should examine the projector to become familiar with how to operate it. Likewise, slide projectors. I have watched many presentations where the speaker pressed the button and what flashed up on the screen was not relevant to the point that was being covered.

A client of mine told me that he experienced the following embarrassing situation. He was giving a talk on his organisation and was using six slides to promote the information. A colleague of his gave a similar presentation but she included three extra slides to cover her area. Because he did not check the slides before he started, he was forced to play around with the remote control until he got back to the slide which was relevant to the point he was covering.

So as part of the preparation always do a dry run of the slides to ensure that they are both relevant to the talk and in the correct sequence.

Some people making presentations may decide to show a video. If the television/video recorder is not one that the speaker normally uses, it is essential to examine it beforehand to see how it operates. This includes identifying how to start it, pause, and raise or lower the volume. It does not look very professional to see the presenter playing around with the remote control. Another thing to remember is to ensure that the tape has been rewound since it was last used. It is not unusual for some presenters to forget to rewind the tape and when they are giving their talk discovering that it is not in order. Once again it undermines the standing of the presenter.

Conclusion

The final aspect of preparation is deciding how to end the talk. A simple way of doing this is to do a short résumé of the main points that were covered so that the audience can leave with the salient issues clear in their minds.

Making the presentation

Body Language: Use of eyes, hands, and legs

It is possible to spend a lot of time preparing for a presentation, yet find that it will fail due to the manner in which it is delivered. This final section will outline how to deliver a talk that will hold the interest of the audience and convey the information in a clear, lively and effective manner. When giving a talk or presentation, it is important to deliver it in a manner that will hold the interest of those who are listening. While the voice of the speaker will contribute greatly to achieving this objective, the use of body language also has a major role to play. This includes the use of eyes, hands and feet.

1. Establishing eye contact with the audience

When addressing an audience it is essential to look around at the group and make everyone feel that they are being spoken to. Many speakers tend not to do this as much as they should and may be looking down at the floor, up at the ceiling or over the heads of the listeners. One of the reasons for this is that the audience may not be giving any reaction to what the speaker is saying. It is important for a speaker to get an indication of what the audience is feeling in relation to what is being said.

Feedback is important and without it the speaker can feel uncomfortable.

There are two main types of reaction that an audience can give. One is very positive. They like the speaker or agree with what is being said and they may be smiling or nodding and this makes the speaker feel good and more at ease. The other reaction is negative. The audience is not giving any reaction and this can make the speaker feel less assured.

Let's say that I am giving a presentation to a group and I find that on one side of the room I am getting a good reaction. On the other side they are staring stony-faced and giving no reaction. It would be wrong for me to ignore that group and spend the rest of my time looking at the group that are giving me a good reaction. The right thing to do would be to maintain eye contact with all the listeners and make them all feel that I am addressing them.

It has often been said that a speaker should pick out one person in the audience and deliver their talk to that individual. I disagree with this. If I were to do that, the person in question may start thinking, "Why is he looking at me all of the time?" and may feel uncomfortable, and the rest of the audience may start to feel left out.

There may be occasions where the audience is so large that it is not possible to establish eye contact with everyone. In this situation the speaker should look across the room to the left, the centre and the right. Maintaining good eye contact is essential.

If acetates are being used, it is essential to maintain eye contact with the audience rather than with the screen. If the speaker spends too much time addressing the screen it can contribute to the audience losing interest, also the speaker's voice will not be projected towards the listeners.

In the section on preparation, I mentioned there are occasions when it is necessary to read a speech word for word. This could be to ensure that a particular message is conveyed. The best way to do this is as follows. Before getting into the detail, the speaker should address the audience in an informal manner looking around as he or she outlines the purpose of the presentation. Then they will start reading from the script. When they reach the end of a sentence or paragraph, they can deliver the last few words looking at the audience, before reverting back to the script again. By putting a mark under the final words it will remind the speaker to establish eye contact for those words.

At the end of the speech when all the information has been conveyed, the speaker can then address the audience to invite them to ask any questions or to thank them for attending the meeting, etc. By doing this, the speaker can get their message across in exactly the manner that they felt was necessary, yet will not bore the audience by reading word for word.

2. Speaking with one's hands

The use of one's hands to liven the delivery and emphasise important words or points contributes to the success of a talk or presentation. For a speaker to stand with their hands lying flat by their side, on their hips, in their pockets or behind their back does not enhance their standing in the eyes of the audience. It can make them look uncomfortable, unsure or ill at ease. Worse still is the speaker who folds their arms in front of their chest. We all like to fold our arms when sitting down or in a relaxed environment talking to people. However, I don't recommend it when standing up before a group. If the speaker is not getting a reaction from the audience they may become somewhat uneasy and if their arms are folded, they may start squeezing them tighter. This could create a hunted look which will undermine their reputation.

So what should one do with one's hands? Speak with them; use them to add expression to the talk. Raise, drop, or expand them depending on the issue that is being discussed. For example, I am recommending to the audience that we should enlarge the membership of our organisation. When I use the word "enlarge", I will widen my hands to demonstrate growth, development or expansion. This will contribute to emphasising the point that I want to stress. Another example would be if I was telling the audience that I was listening to a topic being discussed. I might put my hand behind my ear to emphasise what I had been listening to.

While using the hands to liven the delivery is recommended, it is important not to go over the top and become over dramatic. That could undermine the audience's regard for both the speaker and the subject. Some people will remember Magnus Pyke, who used to appear on television in the 1970s. He used his hands in a strange way. It suited his personality and made him interesting to watch. However, when giving business presentations or representing an important organisation, that would not go down well. The use of hands to stress and emphasise words or issues will enhance a presentation.

3. Stance

The third aspect of body language when giving a presentation is the manner in which the speaker stands. It is not uncommon to see a speaker leaning against a lectern, a hand on a table or chair, knees bent, legs moving in and out, one ankle in front of another. This does not contribute to the image of authority that a speaker should aspire to. While performers in show business will benefit from standing in any way that they wish, making business presentations, or representing an organisation is different. A certain amount of movement is acceptable as it can contribute to a more lively presentation. It would not enhance the speaker if he or she looked like a statue (even a moving one!). Therefore I suggest that the speaker should stand straight, head and shoulders up, looking assured, confident and in control.

To summarise, establish good eye contact with the audience, use one's hands to emphasise points and stand with authority. This will contribute to making a very effective delivery.

4. Voice

As I mentioned, the onus is on the speaker to hold the interest and attention of the audience. Many speakers fail to do this, because their voices are not easy to listen to. The major difficulties that people can have in this area are voices that are low, monotone, lacking in vitality, or that they speak too slowly or too fast. Also, further problems include not putting emphasis on important points, and not using pauses to let important points sink into the minds of the listeners.

While most people do not have bad voices they do have untrained voices. While their voices work well enough when talking to individuals in conversation or sitting around a table at a meeting they do not work well when standing up before a group.

It is my view that there is no such thing as a dull subject; it is the speaker who makes it dull. A ridiculous or crazy topic delivered in a lively, enthusiastic manner will hold the attention of more people than an excellent topic delivered in a dull, monotone voice.

5. Attitude

When addressing a group it is important to speak to the audience, rather than at them. Because people when they are speaking do not know how they are coming across, they may be unaware of the impact that they are creating. There is one word that creates the difference between talking to rather than talking at a group, and that word is "you". To stand up and overuse the word "you" can be misinterpreted by some of the listeners. They may think that the speaker is lecturing them, or even criticising. For example, I am representing a charitable organisation and I am addressing a group to try to persuade them to donate money for a cause. I stand up and say:

"Good evening, ladies and gentlemen. I am here tonight to speak to you about your responsibility to contribute as much as you can to the people living in poverty in the Third World. You are probably reasonably well off individuals, and you have an obligation to assist these unfortunate human beings. I would like you to give an extra ten pounds a month for the rest of this year. This will have a very positive effect on these poor people!"

Because the audience is very conscious of the dreadful situation in some parts of the world, I will probably succeed in getting what I want. However, I may also get a certain negative reaction as some people may resent my attitude. They may see me as talking at them, and implying that they are not very charitable people. I believe it would be far better if I adopted a different attitude and addressed them as follows:

"Good evening, ladies and gentlemen. I am here this evening to talk about our responsibility to contribute as much as we can to people living in the Third World. While most of us are probably not wealthy individuals, we are perhaps amongst the better off members of society and we are very concerned about those unfortunate people. If we were to look at our financial situation and see if we could donate ten pounds a month for the rest of this year, this will make a big contribution to these people in the Third World."

The latter approach would in my opinion be the one to use. The main difference was in using what I call the "royal we". Including myself in what I was asking the audience to do would break down the barrier that may have been erected in the first speech. Whenever one is making a point that could imply a criticism, the use of the words "someone", "one", "people", or "individuals" contributes to building a rapport with those who are being spoken to. Using the word "you" can erect a barrier and this can lead to a negative response, even if it is not articulated. So attitude has a role to play in successful presentations.

6. Humour

By recommending the use of humour when making a presentation, I am not suggesting becoming a joker or telling funny stories. It would not enhance the status of the speaker or the organisation that was being represented if after talking for some minutes the speaker stops and says, "Did you hear the story of the man who went to visit his doctor...?" and told a funny story. It would make the speaker look foolish and cheapen the presentation.

However, thankfully most people have a sense of humour, so a humorous comment or remark will go down well. The longer the talk goes on and the more complex the subject is, the greater the need for a note of levity. A one-liner, or a story that is relevant to the topic being discussed will always be acceptable. A very good way to use humour is for the speaker to tell a story against themselves. To comment on one's idiosyncrasies, habits or shortcomings, makes the audience respond well to the speaker.

There are occasions when humour is not appropriate, for example, when announcing redundancies, or informing the board about a bad investment. However, humour has a role to play in most presentations.

7. Dialogue

The use of dialogue rather than narrative when telling a story or relating a conversation, makes a presentation a lot easier to listen to. Throughout this book all of the conversations that I comment on are told in dialogue. In this chapter, when I outlined my meeting with "Jack" the accountant, I discussed our conversation in dialogue form. I did not say, "I asked him what went wrong". I said, "What do you think went wrong?", etc.

When giving presentations, whenever possible use dialogue to make the presentation more lively.

8. Fluency

The final aspect of making a good presentation is having a good flow of words. Fluency plays a major role in successful speaking. Many people when speaking frequently use two sounds: "em" and "eh".

Often sentences start with "And, eh . . .". This introduces a note of hesitancy and can give the impression that the speaker is unsure of what is coming next. It is in many cases a habit, but if it can be over-come, it makes the delivery of a talk easier to follow.

Another point is the overuse of the same words. In the English language there are approximately 800,000 words but most people use only about ten thousand. They come across words every day in books, papers and magazines which they fully understand but fail to use.

So, when giving a presentation or making a speech, it helps if the speaker can use as many words as possible in order to enhance the delivery.

To summarise on this section, the following are the skills of the good presenter:

1. Being well prepared.

2. Having a good opening.

3. Maintaining good eye contact with the audience.

4. Using one's hands to liven the delivery.

5. Standing straight as a figure of authority.

6. Speaking with a clear, lively voice and putting emphasis on words that need to be highlighted.

7. Talking to rather than at the audience.

8. Using humour where appropriate to enliven the talk.

9. Using dialogue to make the talk livelier.

10. Having a good flow of language.

Good preparation and the ability to deliver the talks well is the first aspect of overcoming one's fear of speaking to a group.

Coping when things go wrong

The second way to overcome one's fear of public speaking is to have the ability to cope with difficult situations and to know what to do if things go wrong.

The ideal situation is for a person to walk into a room to give a speech or a presentation and to know that they could cope with any difficulty that may arise. This will be influenced by their knowledge of what can happen and how to deal with it. The difficulties that can occur when people give a talk are as follows:

1. They get a mental block.

2. Someone interrupts the meeting.

3. A siren is heard.

4. A question is proposed from a member of the audience.
These things can make an inexperienced speaker feel uncomfortable and can affect their speech. Most people who are not experts in an area will fail to perform well when a crisis happens. I tell this story on my course.

In the 1970s, I was very interested in horses. But I had no experience of riding a horse. I had a few friends who were very experienced riders and one Sunday night we were having a drink in Madigan's Pub in Donnybrook. One of my friends said to me,

"Frank, you have often said that you would like to become a good horse rider. Would you like to come with us next Saturday when we will be going riding?"

I had a few drinks taken, so I said "Yes, I would love to."

We agreed to meet on the following Saturday to go for a ride. I left Madigan's feeling very pleased at the prospect of doing what I had wanted to do for a long time. The following Friday I got a call from one of my friends telling me how to get to the stable. Due to the fact that I was sober, and that the event would take place the next day, I began to feel uncomfortable. The idea of getting up on a horse made me feel uneasy.

The next day, I arrived at Killegar in Enniskerry and after I parked my car I met a young stable boy and said to him,

"I am here to ride for the first time and I am feeling very nervous. Could you get me a horse that is very old?"

He brought me around to a stable and said,

"This horse would be ideal for you. He is very easy to control. He is particularly good for children."

I was amazed to hear this, because I was not a child.

He helped me up and for over ten minutes the horse stood very still while my friends mounted. The gate was then opened and twelve of us went out, moving very quietly for a few minutes. I felt very comfortable and sat in a relaxed way.

After about five minutes I heard some movement up front and then saw the first horse starting to canter. The other horses followed suit.

Within a few seconds my own horse started to canter and in fear, I pulled the reins having seen how the cowboys in films used to do it. The horse got a jolt and it threw me off. When I got up off the ground, feeling bruised and sore, I realised the difficulty that I had. I did not know how to cope with a challenging situation.

If one contrasts that with experienced horsemen and women, one can see the difference. They know a lot about horses. They would know things about the horse that they were with every day. They know how to control the difficulties that can occur and even if they are going to be thrown, they know how to fall without doing themselves too much damage. A good public speaker is the same. Things can and do go wrong when one is talking to a group. However, if one knows what can go wrong and how to deal with it, then it is easy to walk into the room feeling relaxed and being able to say, "I don't care what happens now. I know that I will be able to cope with it."

Knowing what to do when things go wrong is the second way to overcome one's fear of public speaking.

The third way to achieve this is to be able to think under pressure, marshal one's ideas and remain in control. To develop this, one needs training in disciplined thinking.

The final way to become a very effective speaker is having plenty of practice and experience. If a person has only very few talks to give each year, then they can retain their uneasiness. However, if one has a lot of talks to make, then they will be able to do it in a relaxed way. When we look at all the things we all do regularly — driving cars, riding bikes, using computers, doing our work, playing sport — it is the case that while things can go wrong at times, we are still able to cope with it.

The final point that I would like to emphasise is the danger of drinking before one makes a talk. Many people attend events such as a wedding, acting as best man, or at a dinner in an organisation or a sports club. While eating they will drink some wine. If they drink too much it can make it more difficult for them to give their talk. On several occasions I had to do such things but I never took a drink until after I did my speech. Much as I like wine when I am eating, I am more committed to making a good speech.

Becoming a good speaker and being able to represent companies and organisations in a professional manner is more important in today's fast-moving business environment than it has ever been before.

11

Conclusion

This book has outlined how a person can gain a good insight into communicating with people and dealing with challenging situations. To become a very self-confident person, a successful public speaker and an expert in communication skills however it is necessary to take part in a training programme.

   Having read this book, the reader should:

1. Have a very positive mental attitude.

2. Have learned how to converse with people in a constructive way.

3. Have a greater insight into how human beings think, act and react.

4. Be better able to cope with individuals who are difficult to deal with.

5. Know how to prepare for and resolve conflict situations.

6. Be able to cope effectively with challenging and difficult situations.

7. Be able to participate in or even chair meetings effectively.

8. Be able to prepare for, structure and deliver presentations successfully.

Appendix A

The story of Frank P. Murphy and Ireland's Institute of Communication Ltd, by Carol O' Boyle, a journalist who took part in Frank's course in 1979. This article was published in the *Sunday Tribune* in September 1995. It outlines how Frank:

Overcame his fear of public speaking;
Developed his skills through opposing his parish priest in 1968;
Won an election by his ability to remember people's names;
Attracts so many private citizens to his course.

On an evening in February, 1968, over a hundred people crowded into a room in Buswell's Hotel, Molesworth Street, Dublin, to attend a debate on the motion "That Dublin Town should come tumbling down", which dealt with the issue of development of the city. When the proposer, a very confident, articulate speaker who had made a fluent, lively and humorous speech sat down to thunderous applause, the chairman rose to introduce the opposing speaker. However, Frank P. Murphy, who was very shy and had a stammer, sat paralysed in his chair, terrified, dumbstruck and unable to move. Eventually, after much encouragement from the chairman, he managed to make a short, faltering speech, which remained inaudible to most of the audience. He lost the debate by a landslide.

Refusing to be deterred by that experience, he went back the following week and said a few words standing at the back of the room. Week after week he pushed himself forward and soon conquered his fear of speaking. Within six months he was teaching young people how to debate and speak in public in the youth club in his local parish. His determination to become an effective speaker was motivated by his ambition to go into politics due to the strong nationalistic background that he came from.

How Frank developed his skills

All of Frank's courses in communication skills come from the practical experience that he developed over many years and from his study of psychology. His first major experience was in the autumn of 1968 in his local parish. The parish priest had built a Parochial Hall and appointed a Parent and a Youth Committee. Frank, who had been a devout altar boy and later a Church Steward, was put on the Youth Committee. Frank was a very good parishioner and had the nickname, "Cardinal Murphy". He was very respectful to the priests. He was very polite and well mannered. He was also very political and was strongly committed to democracy, human rights and equal opportunities for women and people from the working classes. Ireland in the late 1960s had changed a great deal and many young people were involved in left-wing activities. Lots of students in Irish universities were engaged in activities to bring changes to the country. Frank was one of those people.

While he accepted the position on the Youth Committee, he opposed the compositions of both committees on the grounds that all of the members were male and from the middle classes. He believed that women and parishioners from what would have been called the working classes should have been included. He also claimed that future committees should be elected rather than appointed. He set up an organisation called "The Parochial Democratic Movement" and for two years campaigned to achieve his objectives. This meant that he had to make speeches, debate, chair meetings, negotiate with his opponents and resolve conflicts. Frank says "The year was 1968; I was young and very radical. I knew that I had made mistakes but I learned a great deal, gained a lot of experience and developed considerable confidence in myself." To oppose priests in those days was very controversial and unacceptable. However, it did provide Frank with the opportunity to become very successful as a public speaker, as a negotiator, and also at resolving conflicts and influencing and persuading people.

The importance of standards in training

Frank's communications training programme, which he has been conducting since 1972, imparts all of the skills that he developed both academically and practically. He will never conduct a course if he has not got practical experience or professional training in the area. Frank says, "It is very easy to conduct a course by taking pieces out of books or from the notes of other courses if one is training people who know nothing about the subject. For many years I have read economics. I could put together a course by taking bits from the books by Adam Smith, John Maynard Keynes, or John Kenneth Galbraith. To people who know nothing about economics it might be a revelation to them. But to those who are interested in becoming knowledgeable about economics it would be unacceptable. They would need training from a qualified economist."

His skills in winning an election

In 1970 Frank ended his disagreement with his clergy to the satisfaction of both sides and he continued to pursue his political ambitions. A friend of his was auditor of a leading debating society and was coming to the end of his term of office. The debating society was then a very well known organisation, which held debates every fortnight on the major issues facing the country. The speakers invited included the Taoiseach of the day, government ministers, union leaders and people involved in national organisations. It got a lot of media coverage. Frank saw this as an opportunity to become known in order to develop his political career so he decided to stand for election as auditor in October 1970. His big disadvantage was that he belonged to a different debating organisation and he was not well known to most of the voters. He had two candidates opposing him who were better known as debaters by the people who were eligible to vote. The campaign went on for three weeks before the election.

At the end of the first night of the campaign Frank had an interesting thought. He decided that if he could remember the names of the voters on the election night that that might influence them to vote for him. He spent a lot of time that night thinking about how to remember people's names and he devised a way of doing it. For the next twelve nights he greeted the voters, asked them their names and used the system that he devised. On the night of the election his two opponents stood at the entrance to the building greeting the voters and issuing leaflets to them. Frank stood inside the hall and when the voters had passed his opponents he was able to greet many of the people by "their name" and requested their support. He won the election by a large majority. Later that night many voters were asked why they voted for Frank and they said that they were pleased that he had remembered their names.

Frank was delighted and felt that when he stood for election in the Dáil within two years that he could stand at the polling station and greet a lot of voters by name. When he set up his communications skills course in 1972 he found a career that fascinated him and because of the long hours that he had to work he did not have the time to spend in the political party that he was involved in. Throughout the next twenty years he became involved in a number of organisations where he has had the opportunity to make speeches, give presentations, negotiate, resolve conflicts and use many of the skills that he trains people in.

The confidence of the Irish race now

When Frank set up his course all of the people who attended came as individuals as most companies in those days did not regard training in personal skills as a priority. A lot of the companies who were interested in this type of training would not have used a local organisation, with the exception of the IMI (Irish Management Institute), which by then was well established. Frank tells the following story:

"In what I call the bad old days, most Irish people had very little confidence in both themselves and their country. They tended to look to the then more advanced countries throughout the world. They had more confidence in foreign products and would prefer to buy them rather than Irish ones. That is why so many Irish companies failed to develop.

"In the late 1940s, my father was president of the former National Agricultural and Industrial Development Association and he set up the 'Buy Irish' campaign and the 'St. Patrick's Day Parade' to encourage Irish people to buy Irish products. He was a chemist and had a pharmaceutical company. In the 1950s he changed the name of his company to a Dutch one, as Irish people would always be more interested in buying foreign products.

"When I set up my course, I experienced that same attitude. Most Irish companies preferred to send their staff on foreign courses. Thankfully, all that has changed. Irish people are now a lot more confident and are willing to give equal status to an Irish product as they are to products from other countries. The same applies to courses. While there are some very good courses available in other countries and our minds should be open to ideas from all over the world, it is very encouraging that Irish people and companies and now willing to use Irish training organisations."

Why citizens prefer to be trained by Frank

The reason why so many individuals and companies who require training in communication and presentation skills use Frank Murphy is that he became a very good communicator as a private citizen. I agree with Frank's view on what impresses many people. If a person is a well-known figure it is a lot easier for them to make an impact in front of an audience. The fact that they are well known gives them status. Many members of the audience will be impressed with them and will defer to them. When Frank set up his course he was unknown to the public. If he was a well-known personality, a journalist, broadcaster, or even a sportsman, he would have attracted lots of people to his course, regardless of his experience or qualifications. While most of the people who attend his courses are very qualified and experienced, they are private citizens so they prefer to be trained by someone who had to become a good speaker without the advantage of being a public figure.

A Strong supporter of the Arts

Besides his great interests in communication skills training, Frank is a strong supporter of the Arts and has lectured on James Joyce. He is very interested in chamber music and has sponsored some of the world's leading musicians at the Irish National Concert Hall. To celebrate his 20 years in business in 1991, he gave a bursary to a young opera singer under the auspices of the Opera Theatre Company and continued to do that every year. In 1994 he gave a prize in the then G.P.A. Dublin International Piano Competition. For many years he has been on the Board and Committee of the Music Festival in Great Irish Houses. In December, 1994, he was appointed a Governor of the Royal Irish Academy of Music.

The course conducted by Ireland's Institute of Communication Ltd includes:

Communication skills.

Presentation skills.

Negotiation skills.

Interpersonal skills.

Appraisals skills.

Management training skills.

Customer care skills.

Conflict resolution skills.

Supervisory skills.

Training the trainer skills.

Letter and report writing skills.

All of the trainers at Ireland's Institute of Communication Ltd have professional qualifications and practical experience in the areas in which they train.

When people leave Frank's course they are a lot more confident. Frank says that they do not leave as Superman or Superwoman, but they have upgraded their communication skills and have developed a good deal of confidence. However, as time goes on some people can go through a crisis in their lives. They may become ill, they may lose their jobs, their relationships may break down. When things like that happen, people can feel very upset and their confidence could fall down. While Frank is in business to earn a living, he is also very committed to assisting people. On the final night of his courses he informs all the participants that if at any stage in the future they were to go through a crisis and the confidence that they had developed went down, that if they felt that attending the course again would help them to become more self-confident that they will be welcome to attend the course again, totally free of charge.

Every year only a very small number of people have to take up this offer. The people who leave Frank's course feel happy in the knowledge that for as long as his business exists that he is willing to assist them.

Index